His Cup Runneth Over

His Cup Runneth Over

Patricia A Eldredge

Writer's Showcase
San Jose New York Lincoln Shanghai

His Cup Runneth Over

Writer's Showcase
an imprint of iUniverse, Inc.

For information address:
iUniverse, Inc.
5220 S. 16th St., Suite 200
Lincoln, NE 68512
www.iuniverse.com

ISBN: 0-595-22555-1

Printed in the United States of America

Contents

1

As we entered the arena a charge of excitement ran through the crowd, like electricity flowing through a cable. I tried to hide my nervousness and cover the absence of my usual optimism from Jeff. I didn't want him to know how much I was dreading this game.

Whether I'm playing cards or rooting for a team, I've never been a very gracious loser. This time though I wasn't concerned with how I was going to feel if the Islanders lost. Jeff was my worry. There had been another hockey game two years earlier when Jeff had become so despondent he had almost given up his own fight. Death had hovered close that night, and the fear I felt then would haunt me for a long time to come.

There wasn't an empty seat to be found in the Nassau Veterans Coliseum, the home of the New York Islander hockey club. On this afternoon in May, in the year 1980, there were many more fans than the usual fifteen thousand that the building normally seated. Every bit of available wall space was covered with banners and posters with messages meant to spur the team on. Most significant was "**DON'T GIVE UP TILL YOU DRINK FROM THE SILVER CUP.**"

This game could be the ultimate victory. The Stanley Cup, signifying the highest honor in the National Hockey League, would be theirs if they won, if not, they would play a seventh and deciding game in Philadelphia, losing the home ice advantage and lessening their chances of being victorious.

Jeff and I had watched every game for the past three years; the last two we'd been season ticket holders and attended every home game. The road games we either watched on TV, or listened to on the radio, something only a **REAL** fan could do. Everyone who knew Jeff well felt if it hadn't been for his avid interest in sports he would have given up a long time ago He was twenty but not typical of others his age. He suffered from Duchenne Muscular Dystrophy a progressive and usually fatal condition. Sports, especially hockey had become one of the most important things in his life, even though he couldn't participate as a player. He knew every play, every penalty and boisterously directed the play from where he sat. I was sure the players couldn't hear him, but sometimes when they did exactly what he was yelling for them to do, I wondered.

Once in awhile a fan that didn't appreciate his constant commands would bark at him, "Why don't you shut up!" and Jeff would shrink down in his chair for several minutes in embarrassment but would soon be hollering again. Then there were those who enjoyed watching him almost as much as the game. His face would go livid with rage if he felt the referee had overlooked a penalty on the opposing team only to call one on the Islanders. He was a tall slim young man, dark wavy hair, hazel eyes and a fair complexion. He wore tortoise shell glasses that constantly slid down his nose, giving the impression of a little old man peering over his spectacles. He was shy and serious most of the time, but had a subtle sense of humor that hid the discomforts and frustration that were so much a part of his life. The past eight years had been spent in a wheelchair, and each had brought more difficulties to contend with.

As I sat on the folding chair behind his wheelchair in the special section set aside for the handicapped, I tried not to think about the outcome of this game. If I let myself dwell on it a feeling close to panic would grip me. How would he handle another defeat?

The noise in the coliseum was deafening as the teams took to the ice for warm-ups. Billy Smith was the first Islander out, which meant he'd be "in goal".

"Let's get 'em! You guys can beat those bums! Send those clowns back to Philly!" Jeff began his usual tirade. Because of the weakness in his arms he was unable to lift his hands to wave or clap, instead he would jerk his head to accentuate his words. Even that took an enormous effort his entire body straining just to nod his head. The almost unbearable tension silenced me as most nerve wracking situations usually did. Then came Jeff's usual requests, "Could you pull the back of my shirt down? Pull my belt tighter? My glasses?" The last he wouldn't have to verbalize, just a certain glance and an upward movement of his chin would be enough. These entreaties which normally wouldn't have bothered me were now beginning to irritate me, and I just wanted to scream. "Leave me alone!" But I managed to keep my feelings under control and did whatever he asked.

The buzzer sounded, and the players began to shoot loose pucks into the waiting crowd that filled the first few rows of stands. Fans of all ages, hoping to get a closer look at the players, many with cameras and slips of paper or photos of the players for autographing. There would be a mad scramble as each puck sailed over the glass, everyone praying he'd be lucky enough to retrieve one for a souvenir. The last player skated off the ice, and the big machine called the Zamboni came out to resurface it. You could feel the pressure mounting as the fans streamed up the stairs to find their seats. The Zamboni continued circling until the surface was completely covered with a layer of water. As the driver steered his way off the ice the buzzer sounded, which meant the players would return for the singing of the national anthem and the first face-off of the game.

2

SUDDEN DEATH OVERTIME

My worst fears were materializing. *"Oh, no, they look flat. They're just not skating."* and as the Flyers scored first my heart plummeted. Any other time I would have said, "Don't worry they'll come back. It's only the first period, there's plenty of time." But I remained silent, filled with despair. This was ridiculous, here I was witnessing the biggest game of the year, and just praying for it to end. When Denis Potvin tied the score, and Duane Sutter scored the go-ahead goal, I didn't feel much better.

There was just too much time left, and I was afraid of what could still happen. And there was much more to come. The teams exchanged goals, and as the end of the second period neared the Islanders led four to two. It was time for me to get our snacks. We had a regular routine worked out. When 2:30 showed on the time clock I leaned over to the man on Jeff's right and inquired, "Frank, can I get you something?" Reaching in his shirt pocket he would pull out a small wad of bills, and handing me one would say, "Yup, large coke, no ice, please."

If I left then I was usually first in line at the snack bar and back to our seats by the time the second period ended,, thus avoiding the mad rush. As I neared the refreshment stand a familiar voice greeted me, "Hi, Pat." Reaching for a large paper cup the girl behind the counter asked, "What will it be? The usual?" "Yup, large coke, no ice first." She filled the cup, and as she rang up the dollar on the register she asked, "What else?"

"Two hot dogs, a coffee and a small coke, please." She walked to the other end to get the frankfurters, and as she returned she queried, "Well, how do you like the game so far?"

"Please, don't ask! I just wish it were over."

"But why?" Sue asked with a puzzled look on her face. "They're winning."

"I know, but there's twenty whole minutes left, and I don't think I can take the suspense."

"I don't believe it, I've never seen you so up-tight over a game before."

As I walked away I threw over my shoulder, "Believe me, I'm not enjoying this one at all."

Back at our seats I had to help Jeff eat, something he could do by himself at home. A wicker table meant for eating in bed, cut down and set on top of our dining room table, added just enough height to make it possible for Jeff to place his left hand with the fork on top of the right, then with the right he would push up the left so he could reach his mouth. It always tore at me to watch, wanting to offer to help but knowing what little independence he still had was important, and hoping too that the more he used his weakening muscles the longer it would take Muscular Dystrophy to triumph. But at the coliseum there was no table, nothing for him to lean on, so between bites of my hot-dog I would be his hands and arms. When five years earlier, he became too weak to even lift a cup, I began carrying straws wherever we went.

Frank was teasing him again, "What eating again?"

"It's my lunch. You wouldn't want me to starve, would you?"

Frank just laughed. He was one of the many friends we'd made at the games. Afflicted with Hemophilia, using a wheelchair only part of the time, he always sat on Jeff's right and had been a season ticket holder since the birth of the Islander hockey team. He ragged Jeff about his yelling and tried to calm him when he got too agitated with the refereeing.

Then there was Gene, a young man in his late twenties, a Cerebral Palsy victim, who got around on crutches. Gene knew all the statistics concerning the game of hockey but angered Jeff when he found fault with some of the Islander players. "They need your support. How do you expect them to do a good job if their own fans are always on their backs?" This was meant for Gene but directed at me. It wasn't till several years later as his confidence in himself increased that he actually began telling Gene what he thought to his face.

There was Stacy, about eighteen, always smiling, with a ready laugh in spite of the many lengthy stays in the hospital resulting from problems caused by Spina Bifida. "Come on Jeff, I bet I can yell louder than you," she'd challenge. Christopher, fourteen, another Cerebral Palsy victim, who did everything with his feet: operated his motorized wheelchair, typed, wrote and even played ball. A wizard!

Danny, in his early twenties, paralyzed since age thirteen from a fall off a roof. An Islander fan except when they played the New York Rangers, and when he cheered for the Rangers I would tease by threatening to push him, wheelchair and all, over the seats onto the ice.

Not everyone was handicapped, but these were the people we sat with almost every game. For Jeff and I it had been an eye-opener, neither of us realizing till then how many other afflictions there were.

The crowd was frantic as the teams returned to the ice for the final period, but soon fell silent as goals by Dailey and Paddock of the Flyers tied the score. I wished then that I hadn't eaten, because it felt as if the hot-dog was sitting in my stomach howling.

Jeff said optimistically, "Don't worry, there's still plenty of time." I longed to match his hopefulness. The third period ended in a tie, which meant **SUDDEN DEATH OVERTIME.** The first team to score would be the winner.

"How much suspense can a person stand?" I groaned inwardly.

As the overtime began time seemed to stand still. Billy Smith was peppered with shot after shot, then seven minutes into the period Lorne Henning poked the puck to John Tonelli, who along with

Bobby Nystrom raced neck and neck with Dupont and Dailey down the ice. Bobby and John crisscrossed, Tonelli got by Dailey and Nystrom broke for the goal. With a perfectly timed pass Tonelli gave him the puck and it sailed into the net.

Pandemonium broke loose.

I jumped up and down crying, "They did it! They really did it!" before grabbing Jeff in a big hug. Feeling a tap on my shoulder, I turned. Sue's arms encircled me, and she exclaimed, "Why you're crying!"

There was madness all around us, fans screaming, a blizzard of confetti raining from the seats high up in the arena, and the popping of corks from bottles of champagne, brought in happy anticipation by some of the fans. A chant of "We're number one." went up, and the organ blasted "We are the Champions." Sue and I stepped aside as Jeff put his chair in reverse, then Jeff and I headed for the lobby where the freight elevator was located, the only way to get Jeff downstairs to the locker room.

3

THE STANLEY CUP

Some players reacted with tears, others smiles, to the dream come true of almost every Canadian boy, and more and more to many American boys. To be on a Stanley Cup team. Trainers, stick boys everyone connected with the team swarmed onto the ice. Coach Al Arbor hugging each player, who in turn embraced each other, photographers snapping pictures.

But Jeff and I didn't wait to see the Cup hoisted high above their heads and skated around the ice; instead we made our way quickly to the elevator through the deserted lobby. Everyone else was still in their seats, watching or joining in the hoopla all around them.

Never aggressive, I amazed myself when I walked up to the elevator operator and indicating Jeff, said very convincingly, "The Islanders want him downstairs." Without hesitation he told us to get in, and the huge freight elevator plunged downward. Once downstairs, we saw players streaming off the ice, and a mass of pushing, yelling fans trying to force their way after them into the locker room. It felt as if the temperature had reached one hundred and ten degrees, and I was thankful Jeff's chair was heavy enough to withstand the pressing mob. Someone closed the locker room door, forcing the milling crowd back again. I clung to Jeff's chair praying we'd survive this mess. One of the trainers spotted Jeff and by some miracle was able to clear a path to the locker room. Inside wasn't much better, reporters everywhere, trying to get a few words with the players. Families, friends all around, champagne flowed freely, some were drinking it, while others found it being poured over their heads. Someone shoved an empty champagne bottle

9

into Jeff's hand, then a hockey stick. There was laughter and shouting, Everyone embracing those close to them.

As the players spotted Jeff they came one by one to shake his hand, making that night one of the happiest of his life. The first to discover him was Wayne Merrick, who reached down, grasped Jeff's hand and putting his free arm round his shoulders said, "Since the first day I joined the team for practice you've been there. Whenever I turned around, there you were. You never gave up on us no matter how bleak things might have looked."

Next was Bryan Trottier. Touching Jeff's Islander jersey he exclaimed, "See, you brought us luck. When we gave you this shirt I told you to wear it to every game and you did." Jeff was speechless, with that telltale smirk, much like that of a Cheshire cat, revealing how much Bryan's words really meant to him.

It had been October of '79 when Bryan had presented him with that shirt. After every game I would wait with Jeff at the press gate for the players to come up from the locker room. A few days before Jeff's twentieth birthday I had written Bryan a note asking him to spread the word that Jeff's birthday was on the twenty-second. I knew how much a simple Happy Birthday from the players would mean to him. Expecting and wanting nothing more I was embarrassed when Bryan gave him the shirt along with a card signed by all the players.

It is difficult for someone who has never known a Muscular Dystrophy victim like Jeff to realize how little it takes to give them pleasure. It's typical of these special people to get infinite joy from the small things the rest of us take for granted. A verbal birthday greeting would have been sufficient. Not that Jeff wasn't thrilled with the card and shirt, he wore that jersey with pride. And now, Bryan the MVP of the playoffs was telling him he had helped them win the Cup.

Jean Potvin was next, putting an arm around each of us he said, "I love you two. You're great. Never have you shown any doubt in us. Whether we win or lose you wait to give us a word of encouragement."

There was to be more. "Hi, big fella, I want you to know you are a big part of our winning," the coach, AL Arbor.

I found a spot to sit and observe. What an experience for Jeff, to be in the locker room with the Stanley Cup Champs and being told he had contributed to their success.

From where I sat I saw Steve Tambellini leaning over talking to him, and as Jeff came towards me afterwards I could see he was disturbed. "Mom, I feel so bad for Steve. He never got to play in even one playoff game."

"I know, I'm sure he's disappointed, but I think he really is happy for the team."

"Hey, Jeff!" yelled a voice behind us.

As Jeff spun his chair around a flashbulb exploded, and his eyes widened in wonder at the huge silver cup engraved with the names of all those players fortunate enough to have been on one of the winning teams.

◆　　◆　　◆

The crowd had thinned considerably, and the players were headed for the showers. "Let's go back upstairs," I suggested, seeing Jeff was beginning to tire. It had been a long day.

As we moved along the almost deserted lobby we could see many fans still waiting outside.

"You don't mind if we stay a few more minutes? I want to say good-bye to everyone. I'm going to miss them this summer." with a trace of sadness in his voice.

Players and their families began to come up. "Have a nice summer, Jeff. See you in the fall at training camp." Then Jeff remarked to me, "I'm glad I was still here to be a part of this."

Tears threatened to spill from my eyes, knowing what was probably on his mind. His next words verifying it, "You know Bryan said they won the Cup for me, but they did it for Artie too."

Artie, another young man with MD, close to Jeff's age, and like Jeff an avid Islander fan, had been to the last Saturday night game of the regular season, and a few days later we heard of his death.

4

HOME

Instead of our customary excited talk about who played well, what a great save the goalie made, or who had a bad game, we were both lost in thought during the forty minute ride on the Southern State Parkway. I felt completely drained and just wanted to get home and into bed. It had been somewhere around noontime when we left for the game, and now it was eight thirty, and I wasn't looking forward to the chore of getting Jeff comfortable for the night.

"Are you hungry?" I tossed over my shoulder to Jeff who sat directly behind me facing the side doors of the van. A seat belt across his chest which was fastened to the back of the driver's seat on one side and a large hook on the other side along with the brakes on his chair held him secure when the van was in motion.

"Let's stop at Burger King. I know you won't feel like cooking when we get home."

"You're so right. Sounds like a good idea to me." Once in Bayshore I drove to Burger King and went in to get hamburgers, fries and cokes to take home.

As we turned in the driveway a few minutes later I said with a deep sigh, "It's great to be home again."

"After we finish eating could we see if the news is on? They'll probably show them skating around the ice with the Cup."

"Sure," I answered as I turned off the motor and made my way back to unhook him. After releasing the brakes on his chair, I lifted the small table that was set in the floor just beyond where he sat and between the two long bench-like seats facing each other. Putting the tabletop on one of the seats I then pulled the tube-like base from its holder and placed that on top of it. Then while Jeff maneuvered his chair around I went outside behind the van, opened the doors and unhooked the hydraulic lift that was fastened just inside. I pulled it out and down, pushed the "raise" button, and the platform began to slowly inch its way up till it was just about an inch below the van floor. Sluggishly Jeff backed his chair towards the open doors, "Am I too far to the left? Am I going straight?"

"No you're just fine. Keep on coming." Trying to keep the impatience from creeping into my voice.

When he reached the lift it took an enormous effort for him to bend enough to fit through the doors. When I bought the van I'd had the original roof removed and a high fiberglass top added. Though the added height didn't make it any easier to get in and out it did make it more comfortable for Jeff while riding and made it easier for me to move around when it was time to unload him. I called the van my 'cup cake" because it looked like a giant cake with a mountain of white icing piled on top. A big plus when I parked in a large parking lot. It was impossible to misplace. Once Jeff's chair was completely on the lift I put on the brake nearest me and pushed the "down" button. Quickly the lift plunged with Jeff on it to the cement below. Reaching down I released the brake on Jeff's chair and after he backed off and out of the way I folded the lift back in place.

Jeff headed up the ramp to the front door with me close behind, stopping just short of the door so I could squeeze by to open it. He drove into the entryway we called the "mud room, and I took the key from the plastic caddie on the arm of his chair to unlock the inside door. Once in the hallway we were greeted by three leaping, yapping balls of white fur, our poodles.

I followed Jeff as he steered his chair down the hall, through the kitchen, into the dinette, where I emptied the bag from Burger King on the table. Then I unlocked and opened the back door to let the dogs out.

When I finished my hamburger I went into the living room and turned on the TV. Jeff directed his chair into position in front, and I went about clearing the table.

Suddenly he shouted, "Come quick, its Denis with the Cup. Wow! It's really something, isn't it? I can't believe I actually touched it."

I stood behind him watching, goose bumps on my arms. It was hard to believe we'd been there.

"I'll watch the weather while you finish cleaning up." said Jeff, "Then to bed."

I went into the kitchen, but there wasn't much to do. Jeff's younger sister Liz had cleaned up everything before she went to work. A senior in high school, she had just bought her first car and was working as a waitress on weekends to pay for the insurance and buy gas. She had wanted to go to the game badly and was going to be really disappointed to hear she'd missed being in the locker room.

Our house was a one-story ranch-type building, decorated in early American, pine paneling in almost every room, with colonial style wallpaper, and accessories to match, many made by Jeff's dad in his workshop in the basement.

Originally the house had been very small and box like, a living room, one fair-sized bedroom, a small bedroom, a tiny bath and a kitchen just large enough to hold a table and chairs, while leaving just enough room to prepare meals.

The house had grown steadily over the years, and just before Jeff was born a larger bedroom and the dinette had been added. The two older boys had taken over what had been the master bedroom, and the small one became Jeff's. When Liz arrived her father built an extension across the full length of the back of the house, adding a large living-recreation room and another bath that doubled as a laundry.

A wall creating a hall going to the front door turned the original living room into another bedroom, and the front and back "mud rooms" were added last by enclosing the cement stoops.

The house appeared normal, "lived in", basically clean but there were differences; the extra table on the dinette table, the scarred woodwork, especially around the doors, and on days when the ground was wet Jeff would leave tire marks of mud or sand on the floors.

"Can't you wipe your feet when you come in? Look at the mud." I'd tease as I cleaned it up.

"Don't be dumb, Mom," he would admonish with that telltale smirk.

◆   ◆   ◆

Jeff had turned off the TV and was ready to go to bed. His room left little doubt as to where his interests lay. The double windows facing westward towards the street were surrounded by shelves holding books, autographed baseballs, a large autographed picture of Jerry Lewis, and bowling trophies. On the south wall was a built-in bed, above which hung an Islander poster and a latch hook piece, the Islander emblem, a present made by Pat Crawford, the next door neighbor. Along the east wall was a long counter top with a small shelf above, displaying pictures, hockey pucks, and statues of hockey players in all shapes and materials.

The paneled walls held banners from the Mets, Knicks, and Islanders. There was another latch hook hanging, made by Jeff himself, designed by his sister, featuring Mike Bossy's number twenty-two in dark blue and two tan hockey sticks crossed in front, on a white background. Next to his bed, underneath the counter were two shelves with record albums and a battery charger for his wheelchair. The counter continued to the corner, then around to the door and held a tropical fish tank, telephone, record and tape players and a lamp shaped like a dolphin.

The opening underneath, except for a small built-in cabinet near the door was empty, giving Jeff plenty of leg room and the vacant top, desk space.

Islander colors dominated the room, the floor carpeted in blue, a blue and white afghan covered his bed and in each of the windows were hung macrame' plant hangers, one in orange, the other blue. The room's proximity to the front door made it the logical one for Jeff, in case of fire. He had switched rooms with Liz when the wheelchair became a necessity.

◆   ◆   ◆

The nightly ritual began. First I removed Jeff's Islander jersey and his sport shirt, then his shoes and socks and the chain he wore around his neck with a silver number one on it. Next I half lifted, half dragged him onto his bed, removing his pants. He slept on his back, his legs now permanently bent, A pillow had to be placed between his legs and his wheelchair on one side and the afghan tucked between another pillow and the wall on the other side because his legs hurt if they fell to either side during the night.

"Could you move my head towards the wall? Pull the pillow down a little?" he asked

Once he was comfortable I plugged in his motorized wheelchair into the battery charger, and that into the wall outlet. As I turned out the light he remarked tiredly, "Night, Mom. This has been the greatest. But I'm exhausted. See you in the morning."

"Good night, you can sleep late. There's no place we have to go tomorrow."

When I finally crawled into bed I found sleep an elusive thing and lay there thinking of all that had happened that day. When sleep still would not come I found my thoughts going back to where it all began.

5

A BIRTH AND A REBIRTH

October 21st, 1959 was a beautiful Indian summer day with no hint of winter in the air, but in the next few days that was to change, as was my life. I began to wonder how much truth there was in the words I'd repeated so many times to my two sons, Billy and Bobby. "Something good comes from everything, no matter how bad it may seem at the time."

By ten-thirty that night all signs indicated it was time for the birth of my third child. Everything pointed to a normal, swift delivery until I was settled in the labor room at Southside Hospital, then all came to a halt. I lay in the stark white, antiseptic smelling room watching the hands on the clock inch slowly towards each approaching hour, through the night.

Was I going to lose the baby? What if I died? Who would care for my family? Such thoughts chased through my mind as I lay there filled with apprehension. Waiting.

Unfortunately my doctor was away, and I couldn't bring myself to question anyone, always too timid to speak up. I watched other expectant mothers come and go on to the delivery room, and with each departure my fears increased

When morning finally arrived the attending physician came to my bedside, "Young lady, I think we've waited long enough for this child. With your permission I'd like to induce labor."

"Please, do something." I pleaded.

Looking back years later I'd wonder if that had been an omen? *Even at birth he needed a helping hand*

By noontime Jeff made his debut into this world. I was relieved and thankful. Even though he was my third son. Some expected me to be disappointed because he wasn't a girl, but I wasn't. To me there was something very special about this baby. Whether it was because of the fear-filled night or something else I couldn't have been happier. Like his brothers he was born with a thatch of raven hair, his was to remain dark like his father's while the others had turned blond like me.

When it was time to bring Jeff home, the phenomena of summer changing to fall had occurred, swirling leaves of yellow, red and brown cascaded down from the thinning trees with each burst of air, a reminder winter would soon be upon us.

The change in me was more subtle. Worry seemed to vanish over the trivial things. Jeff's progress was slow, and instead of worrying I enjoyed each new accomplishment to its fullest no longer caring if someone else's baby was advancing more quickly. When Jeff wasn't walking by the time he reached his first birthday it didn't bother me like it would have in the past. He scurried around the house in a walker, and I just felt he'd walk when he was ready. A few days after his first birthday I was sitting at my sewing machine working on a pair of black pants for Bobby, part of a Chinese costume for Halloween. Jeff had just gotten up from his nap and was wheeling around the house, when suddenly there was a frightened scream, followed by loud wailing. While Jeff had been sleeping I'd gone down to the basement to put clothes in the washing machine. In my haste to get back to my sewing I inadvertently left the door open. Now Jeff lay twisted in his walker, nose, arms and legs scrapped and bleeding, at the bottom of a flight of a flight of cement stairs.

A frantic trip to the hospital followed, where an examination and x-rays showed no injuries aside from the obvious scrapes and bruises. Later his eyes would blacken.

"Don't let him sleep too long, wake him every couple of hours and call me immediately if one pupil appears larger than the other, or he becomes nauseous." Cautioned the Doctor. "They're signs of a concussion. Forty-eight hours should tell the tale."

I spent the next couple of days filled with uneasiness, but aside from the visible scrapes and black eyes, there seemed to be no other after affects.

But as his second birthday neared a feeling of anxiety began to set in, and during his regular checkup I questioned the doctor, "Do you think there is anything wrong? Shouldn't he be walking by now?"

"My children walked late. It doesn't mean a thing. That fall down the stairs could have frightened him so he's afraid to let go. Just give him time." He reassured me.

Jeff finally did walk, and I was so relieved that his unusual gait and the exaggerated way he swung his arms didn't alarm me. He looked so robust and healthy, not fat, but solid and muscular.

"He's going to be a football player, you wait and see," was the prediction.

Like his walking other accomplishments were slow too.

"You do too much for him, he's just lazy," those close to us claimed, blaming me.

He was such a joy and helping him was easy. How quickly they grew independent.

Then I learned I was pregnant again. "It's the best thing for all concerned," was the general consensus.

"With a new baby you won't be able to do so much for Jeff."

On February 3, 1962, not long after my arrival at Southside our daughter made her entrance in this world, quickly, without hesitation. Dr. Bernhardt announced, "Bill will have to add another room for his one, you can't put her in with the others. But I'll tell you this, she will be easier."

Bill had always claimed that it didn't matter that we had only boys, but now his reaction belied his words. On my return home I found the house plastered with signs, "It's a Girl", "At last", "I finally did it." That stung, as if I had no part in all of it.

I had tried to be the perfect wife and mother, keeping the house sparkling, having dinner always on time, washing, ironing, baking pies, cookies and cakes, always trying to please. But all I ever heard was, "You girls are all the same. All you do is watch TV all day."

The large party to celebrate Liz's arrival a couple of days later only added to my depression. I was tired, unhappy and didn't feel like entering into the festivities. But in the weeks ahead those feelings slowly vanished as I enjoyed this little baby girl.

Bibbit Ann, as Jeff called her didn't linger long in infancy, by eight months she was not only walking but running. A tiny blonde whirlwind, who by her first birthday appeared to be the elder of the two.

As time passed I tried to rationalize away the fears that were growing stronger. *Girls are different, they learn faster.* But the speed with which Liz progressed only increased the apprehension.

"Are you sure there is nothing wrong?" I questioned the doctor during each checkup.

"No two children are alike. It's not fair to compare them, he scolded.

The summer before Jeff reached his fifth birthday I decided not to enter him in kindergarten till the following September. He'd have two strikes against him if he started sooner, besides being slow, he would have been one of the youngest. Another year could make such a difference.

6

A COMPARISON

Our house was situated on the eastern side of Saxon Avenue, the borderline between the towns of Bay Shore and Islip. To our south lived Dotty and Tony, a childless couple in their early forties. Tony worked for LILCO, Long Island Lighting Co., as did my husband, Bill. Tony as a welder, Bill in customer service.

Tony was a tormented man, filled with feelings of inferiority caused by the circumstances of his birth and childhood, not knowing who his parents were and being raised in an orphanage. Although his education was minimal he tried to impress people by using big words, often ones he made up himself. "That new shop steward makes me sick, he thinks he's so higigantic," he'd complain.

He was good-hearted, always ready to lend a helping hand. He resented Dotty's large, tight-knit family and the time she spent with them. She was especially close to her mother and would do her shopping for her. Even though she would be home when he returned from work he'd be upset because he knew she'd been there.

Dotty and Tony were at our house almost every night. On one such occasion, over coffee, they mentioned going to the new roller rink just around the corner, and Tony asked Bill, "Why don't you go skating with us one night?"

"They are starting group lessons, and you can learn to skate backwards and do the dances," added Dotty.

"I'm too busy. I've got too many things to do," answered Bill gruffly.

"Would you mind if I went with them?" I asked timidly.

"Go! I don't care," he snapped.

I was disappointed that he refused to go, hadn't we met at a roller rink? I did go in spite of feeling self-concious and nervous and joined the group lessons. I loved to skate and had always wanted to learn how to dance on them. So Tuesday nights became our weekly skating nights. The three of us would go, take the lesson, practice for a couple of hours, then go home for coffee and cake with Bill.

He would listen silently to remarks such as, "Don't you feel stupid skating around holding your arms up like they showed us?" "Do you understand what they mean by edges?"

One night during coffee Tony told Bill, "A real good skater asked Pat if she'd be his dance partner. He's really good, knows all the dances."

With that Bill decided he might be able to find time to go with us.

I was hopeful, so far marriage wasn't what I'd expected. I'd grown up in the days of "and they lived happily ever after" movies and had no idea what marriage really was. My father had died before my second birthday, leaving my mother with my two sisters, an older brother and me. The closeness I longed for in my marriage just wasn't there. When Bill talked, which was only when he was with his brother and his wife or his cousins, it was about things they did as youngsters. Never did he mention his mother who'd died of cancer when he was a teenager. From what I'd gathered from other family members and from his reactions to me, I wondered if her death had some connection with his now apparent hostility towards most females. At the time she died he had been at an age when a boy would be breaking away, and I speculated about whether her death had left him riddled with guilt?

He had drawn the lines in our relationship, he felt earning the money and doing his many projects around the house was all he was required to do, and the children were my responsibility. I tried every way I could think of to get him involved but it was always, "I'm too busy."

Now my hopes rose, if we skated together maybe things would improve, but I was so wrong. He couldn't relax and skate for pleasure; it had to be work. If I so much as talked to anyone, he'd crab, "Come on, let's practice." While Tony's crutch was alcohol, Bill's was work.

I thrived on being among people and skating. But if I so much as talked to anyone he'd drag me away, ranting at me, "We came to learn to skate, not socialize."

We could not even agree on how to practice. "You have to get the steps down pat and then you can worry about the timing," he'd insist.

"How can we keep from tripping each other if we're not doing the same steps at the same time? You have to learn the timing, steps and pattern from the start if you're going to practice with a partner," I argued. But to no avail.

It wasn't long before I began finding excuses not to skate, was too tired, my legs hurt, or I'd take the younger two and concentrate on them. Before Liz was two she put on her first pair of skates and had no trouble standing, but cried when she lost sight of me. So in the beginning her trips to the rink were few and far between. We continued going, Bill even purchasing expensive skates, but I skated less and less.

When Liz was three and a half we began taking her and Jeff more often. Billy was now fourteen and Bobby eleven, neither of them showing any interest in skating then.

It was suggested I put Liz in the Saturday morning group lessons, where she could learn to fall properly, skate backwards and do "shoot the duck", skating on one foot while in a squatting position, one leg extended straight in front held up by both hands. Both Liz and Jeff were eager to begin lessons.

It wasn't long before their teacher, a young teenage girl, came to me with a question," Would you mind if we moved Liz to the more advanced group?"

"No, go ahead," I agreed, sensing there was something more.

"I was afraid it might upset you if we moved her ahead of her brother. After all, he is older than she is."

I felt another twinge of uneasiness but couldn't hold Liz back because of Jeff and knew he wouldn't object. In fact, he jumped at the chance to discontinue his lessons.

"I don't really like taking them, it makes my back hurt," he complained.

I got so much enjoyment out of watching Liz, as did many others at the rink, so tiny, so eager to learn. She soon progressed to the most advanced class and was winning every "shoot the duck" contest held at the end of each lesson. With each win she was presented with an "American On Wheels" pin.

My anxiety over Jeff continued to grow, the skating intensifying my fears, and each time I questioned the doctor his answers didn't satisfy me. It was then I made a decision.

Without a word to anyone but Dotty, my potential baby-sitter, I made an appointment with a bone specialist thinking, *if Jeff needs corrective surgery there'll be plenty of time to recuperate before he enters school. Believing I was* facing up to the worst scenario.

7

A DIAGNOSIS

On a blustery cold day in January I bundled Jeff and Liz up for the ride to Dotty's mother's where Liz and Dotty would wait while Jeff and I kept our appointment. We passed people walking briskly along, hands jammed in their pockets, and in spite of the warmth of the car I felt as cold as they looked. It was fear.

After dropping Dotty and Liz off, Jeff and I proceeded to the doctor's office, where in the waiting room I saw young and old with casts covering various parts of their bodies, and pictured Jeff in one, maybe even bedridden for months. The vision of him running like other children flashed through my mind. It would be worth anything. When it was our turn to go into the inner office another chill shot through me, even though the room was extremely warm, and at the doctor's request I removed Jeff's shoes, shirt and pants, thinking how very healthy he looked. But after a couple of commands, "See those stairs Jeff? Would you climb them for me? And "Sit down on the floor. Now let me see you get up again," the doctor turned and walked towards the door rubbing the back of his neck, then stunned me with the announcement, "He has Muscular Dystrophy."

All that meant to me was that was the disease Jerry Lewis worked so hard to find a cure for. I'd never watched his telethon, but I'd seen those cardboard containers displayed in different places with quarters and dimes in them, and Jerry's picture on the front with some small child in braces or in a wheelchair. Diseases had always frightened me, was afraid to read about them for fear I'd find I had the symptoms they described.

Jeff was happily pulling himself up the stairs again, oblivious to anything else, as the doctor continued, "He might be lucky and stay just as he is, or a cure might be found before it's too late. The researchers say it's just around the corner. But if neither of these happens he'll get steadily weaker until he needs a wheelchair, probably by the time he's twelve. It's doubtful if this happens that he'll live past his mid-teens. There's nothing I can do for him so don't bring him back to me." if he said more I don't remember. He left the room then, leaving me alone to dress Jeff. Somehow I managed to get his clothes back on him and drove him back to pick up Liz. All that was going through my mind was, *My beautiful,, loving child was doomed, and there was nothing I could do about it.*

The remainder of that afternoon is still a blur, just as the three days following the death of my mother. For the first time I was thankful she was gone, not faced with my pain.

The two older boys came home from school and went about their usual activities without sensing anything was amiss. Jeff and Liz were playing in Jeff's room. All I recall was sitting at the dinette table over an untouched cup of tea with Dotty, waiting for Bill and Tony to get home from work.

When I finally heard the slam of car doors I flew into a panic, ran into the bedroom, shutting the door behind me. Then stood staring out the window, seeing nothing, my mind in a quandary, wondering how I could break the news to Bill. I knew this was going to be very difficult for him, especially since Jeff was the son who looked most like him. Up till now he wanted no part of the children's problems and had made it clear I was to handle any that did occur. It wasn't till years later that I learned the reason for his attitude.

Billy, the oldest, was a very serious, nervous child, and when he was seven I consulted the doctor about a bed wetting problem. At the doctor's request I had convinced Bill to go with me to his office.

"There's too much pressure being put on him. One of you is going to have to ease up. Give him some breathing space."

I knew it would have to be me. I wasn't the strict disciplinarian like his father, but in my own subtle way I'd let Billy know I expected nothing short of perfection from him. I knew Bill would never let up so it had to be me, but because I'd asked the doctor for advice, Bill was infuriated. He continued his tyranny, "Have Billy pull the weeds in the driveway, every one of them, before I get home." There was always the threat of a whipping with his belt hanging over him. He insisted Billy clean up after him when he was working on some project, such as adding a room on the house,. "Why doesn't he let me help with some of the work? All I ever do is clean up the mess he makes."

The other three were ignored as far as discipline was concerned unless they were doing something that annoyed him.

Years later Bill told me, "You dragged me to the doctor so he could tell me I wasn't handling my son right, so I decided you could do the worrying over the others."

He built a wall around himself, one I couldn't scale or penetrate. I didn't know how I could cope with what lay ahead if this barrier remained. *How could I face this alone?*

I heard the back door close and Tony's voice, "Hi Dot, where's everyone?"

"The boys are outside somewhere, and the little ones are playing in Jeff's room. Pat's in the bedroom. She's a little upset."

"What's wrong? She didn't have an accident with the car, did she?" snarled Bill.

"No nothing like that."

"Then what's wrong? Annoyance creeping into his voice.

"You'll have to ask her."

I heard the doorknob turn and felt tears threatening, but was determined not to let the fall.

"What's going on?" came Bill's voice behind me. Forgetting my intention of trying to ease some of the shock, I blurted out, "It's Jeff. I've been worried about the trouble he has running so I took him to a specialist today. I still can't believe what he told me. Jeff has Muscular

Dystrophy. He's going to die. By the time he's twelve he'll probably be in a wheelchair, and there's nothing we can do about it." I reached out for some sign of support, but my hand remained empty.

Then the tears fell.

"Stop it!" he said harshly. "I'm leaving if you're going to carry on. I don't want to hear anymore." As suddenly as they started the tears stopped, numbness creeping in. I was to look back years later and think, *He might as well have left me that day.*

Then I heard Dotty's voice from the other room. "Dr. Bernhardt's on the phone and wants to talk to you. I glanced towards Bill, and when he made no move, went into the kitchen and took the receiver in my shaking hand.

"Pat, are you all right?" I could hear the deep concern in his voice. "Dr. Hall called me right after you left his office. We have to talk. Can the two of you come to my office at seven?"

"Yes, I have so many questions. We'll be there." *He will get Bill to face it.* I thought hopefully.

But at the office Bill sat silently by while the doctor and I talked.

"Did you know?" was my first question.

"No, to be perfectly honest with you, I had no idea. In my twenty years as a doctor I've never had a patient with MD. I really thought he was just slow. But I don't want you to go by one diagnosis. This is much too serious. I want you to make an appointment with Dr. Leon Cherish, who specializes in these things."

"But if its true, can't he fight it?"

"There is no way to beat this. You're going to have to accept it."

I didn't want to believe him *Hadn't I heard of people with supposedly incurable conditions who survived in spite of what the doctors predicted?* "Will he suffer much?"

"My advice to you is not to look ahead. There are going to be dark days. Try to make the most of the time he has. It isn't going to be easy but sharing will help lesson the pain."

I turned and looked towards where Bill had been sitting, but the chair was empty. He was staring out the window, his back to me.

8

WAITING

The next six months waiting for an appointment with Dr. Cherish, were the worst I've ever had to live through, my emotions dead to everything but the pain I felt for Jeff. I went through the motions of living, even forcing myself to give Liz a party for her third birthday.

I tried not to think ahead but watching Jeff with a new awareness made that difficult. How easily he fell, and what a Herculean effort it took for him to get back on his feet. All the things I'd ignored or minimized were so painfully obvious now. There were days when I was sure the doctor was wrong, but more when I was positive he wasn't. They were lonely months of torture.

Often on his way to the hospital Dr. Bernhardt stopped by to see us, his distress apparent.

I had always loved the change in seasons, thrilled at the first snowflake, rejoiced at the sight of daffodils poking their leaves through the cold ground, but now I felt nothing but despair.

At our first social outing after learning the devastating news about Jeff, one young mother sure she had all the answers gave me some unsolicited advice, "What you should do is have him put away somewhere. You have to consider the rest of the family. It's not fair to them to have to live with this."

This angered and upset me and I fled to the ladies room in an attempt to recover my shattered composure. When I returned to our table I avoided her.

On our way home, needing reassurance and not yet willing to concede I wouldn't get it from Bill, I said, "Betty thinks we should put Jeff away somewhere."

When there was no reaction, fear shuddered through me, and I thought, *Maybe he agrees with her.*

◆   ◆   ◆

When we arrived at Dr. Cherish's office in June my impression of him was the exact opposite of the way I felt about the doctor who made the first diagnosis. In the months after that first diagnosis I almost hated him for what had seemed like cold and unsympathetic behavior. Not an unusual reaction, I was told.

Even though Dr. Cherish agreed with him he tried to show us the bright side. "These children are very special. What they lack in capabilities they make up for with love. Don't run from doctor to doctor. There is no help yet. Accept it and make the most of every day you have with Jeff."

I left with a seed of hope. I didn't want a picture of the future drawn for me, I was still too cowardly for that, but if Jeff's life was to be a short one I vowed I would do what I could to make it a good one.

I might have gone overboard and done too much for him, but there were things that made me pause and think. The other children needed help in coping with what lay ahead, and I recalled my own childhood restricted to the house months on end, because of complications from ear infections, feeling the resentment, real or imagined over the extra attention my sisters felt I received, when all I wanted was to be treated like everyone else. *Why should Jeff feel any different?*

The Patient Coordinator from the Muscular Dystrophy Association assured me, "You'll get everything Jeff needs in the way of braces, lifts, and wheelchairs from us, at no cost to you. He'll have an annual evaluation at the MD clinic, and as far as advice on how to treat him, try to keep things as normal as possible. Don't be impatient and do things he's capable of doing himself just because it takes him longer. Just remember, if you spoil him, and a cure is found, you'll spend the rest of your life running to psychiatrists trying to straighten him out."

The usual question came to my lips, "Will he suffer much?"

"Physically he'll have some discomfort at times, but psychologically you will suffer more. These children accept what's happening better than we do. You will think of all the things he can't do and ache for him. But like someone who wears glasses, he'll adjust to his limitations."

My morning period was over, life had to be faced and dealt with. I managed to keep things going as usual, and the two older boys wrapped up in their own lives didn't notice the anguish in me.

◆　　◆　　◆

Now it was time to explain to his brothers what was happening to him. After clearing away the dinner dishes one evening, Billy washing, Bobby and Jeff drying, I followed the two older boys into their room. Taking a seat on the lower bunk, I began, "Your father and I took your brother to see a specialist. You know how hard it is for him to run? We wanted to find out if anything could be done to help him. But there is nothing the doctors can do. Jeff has a muscle disease called Muscular Dystrophy. It weakens his muscles, till one day he'll have to use a wheelchair."

"But you can see how strong his muscles are in his legs." Protested Bobby.

"I thought the same thing, but the doctor says no. The reason his muscles are so large is because they have to work twice as hard as your normal muscles do."

"Can we get it too?" asked ever fearful Billy.

"No, it would have shown up by now."

"What about Bit?" asked Bobby, referring to his sister.

"No, she's safe. This type only affects boys. She could be a carrier though, which means when she is older she could have babies with it."

"You mean you gave it to Jeff?"

"No, no one is to blame. I didn't know I was a carrier, but that's not important. What we do is. It'll be a long time before he's in a wheelchair. Meanwhile I want you to treat him as you always have, and if you have any questions I'll try to answer them."

I left them then hoping I'd said the right things. *They'll know soon enough how serious it really is.*

9

SUMMER'S GROWTH

The summer months were filled with trips across the bridge spanning the Great South Bay to Robert Moses State Park, with almost everyone enjoying themselves, drinking in the sunshine, frolicking in the ocean. Jeff loved the water but didn't venture out to where the waves were breaking, afraid of being knocked down. Instead he ran like in a walking race along the edge of the shore or just lay on his stomach where the water gently lapped over him like a caress.

As for me, I was crying inside.

Many of those excursions were with the Klecan family, one of the few living on Saxon Avenue when our house was built in 1954. Mary and Joe, their four sons Barry, Ronnie, Johnny and Joey. A fifth son was born a few year later, Robert Peter. Everyone call him Petey, and when I asked why he didn't go by his first name his mother replied, "Robert just didn't fit, it was too formal."

He was to become a big influence in Jeff's life as the years passed, but that summer he was just one of the gang, more Bobby's friend than Jeff's.

When it was too cool to go to the ocean I took Liz, Jeff, Petey and Bobby to the school playground to romp on the monkey bars, slide, swings and merry-go-round, a welcome challenge for Jeff then. I watch skittishly as he climbed to the top of the monkey bars, wanting to warn him of the danger, but knowing I couldn't spoil what he could still do with my fears.

Bobby turned twelve that July and was finally old enough to have a much longed for paper route like his brother. I cursed <u>Newsday</u> when there a few papers missing and a battle would ensue over whose was short. Bill, angrily reprimanded Billy for leaving the wires that held the bundles together carelessly on the ground.

With money earned from his route, Billy bought a "Slip-N-Slide", a yellow strip of plastic about ten foot long and two foot wide over which a constant stream of water flowed from the garden hose. They would run and slide ending up on their backsides. Jeff liked it too even though it was a struggle to get back up on his feet at the end. Another favorite pastime for Jeff, Bobby and Petey was playing with Bobby's Playschool Village. A canvas bag spilled forth blocks of various shapes and sizes for building houses, churches, a firehouse and stores. There were even tiny wooden cars and trees. The large canvas square with streets, sidewalks, lawns and parking lots would be laid on the floor or the ground and they would build a whole town, adding their "matchbox" cars they would play for hours.

To our north lived the Cummings. Jay, an only child, spent his free time between our house and Klecan's. The four older Klecan boys, along with Jay and Billy played baseball almost every evening after supper in the vacant lot next to the Klecan house.

We all watched Jeff that first summer after the doctors' diagnosis with a mixture of love and pain, each wishing we could somehow give him some of our vitality, not knowing as his muscles withered a different kind of strength was growing in him and me.

10

SCHOOL

Jeff had to be up extra early in the mornings when school began in the fall because it took so long to dress himself. It would have been easier and quicker to help, but the words of the man from Muscular Dystrophy echoed in my mind. After breakfast I walked to the bus stop with him, and watched as he struggled up the steep steps onto the big bus. Kevin, a boy from our neighborhood was starting kindergarten too, so Jeff had someone he knew to sit with during the ride. He left each morning with a big smile on his face and returned still beaming at the end of the day, waving his work proudly, like a banner.

His biggest fear was getting knocked down in the crowded classroom since it was so difficult for him to get up again. To do this he would grip his legs with his hands near his ankles, and "walk" his hands up them, till his body was upright.

He loved school and his report card showed no unusual problems for a child in his first year. He was immature and extremely shy, not unusual for someone in kindergarten.

He stood proud and happy in his diminutive cap and gown on graduation day months later, and if I could go back and relive our lives from that day on, things might have been different.

◆　　　◆　　　◆

For Bill's vacation that year we drove to the farm the Cummings were planning on retiring to in a few years, in Salem, New York, and on the way we stopped at the Catskill Game Farm.

"Oh, Mom, look at those baby deer. Can we feed them?" Liz was jumping up and down even though she had been car sick almost the entire drive.

"Dad, can we take a ride on the little train over there?" asked Bobby pointing to it as it chugged around the mountain.

Even though there were no steep inclines where we were walking it was treacherous for Jeff, and he clung to me to keep his balance on the uneven ground. I was thankful when we continued on our way, and fortunately Liz wasn't sick the remainder of the trip.

◆   ◆   ◆

The country surrounding the farm was beautiful, mountains covered with trees, valleys green and wide, a farmhouse dotting the landscape here and there, and crystal clear streams of water. Fog shrouded the mountains about halfway up, the tips reappearing again high above. Bill loved it and talked of moving there permanently, while silently I objected.

I saw how laborious it was for Jeff to climb the hill behind the farmhouse when we were searching for the neighbor's cows that Mr. Cummings told us would be grazing in the pasture beyond and how coming back down proved even more difficult. A farmhouse would become a prison for Jeff.

We drove around the countryside visiting old forts and used furniture lots. Historic sights held no excitement for me, but the children climbed on the old cannons, pretended they were being punished in the stockades, and scrambled aboard the ancient railway cars, as if embarking on some great adventure.

After growing up with nothing but mismatched furniture, browsing through piles of junk looking for some treasure left me cold and wasn't my idea of how to spend a vacation. Nevertheless Bill had to stop whenever he saw a sign reading "Antiques"

I was relieved when we returned home and could see Jeff was glad to be back. Before summer ended he learned to ride a two-wheeler, but he needed the assurance that the training wheels were there.

We bought a tent for the older boys, who along with Jeff and the neighborhood children, took turns sleeping out in the Cummings' lot where they had let us set it up.

When September came Jeff went into first grade, and it was then that I began to wonder how much I should expect from him? I felt I needed guidance and unfortunately turned to the school psychologist.

My track record being a mother, in my opinion, wasn't the best. *Hadn't I helped make Billy extremely nervous with my unrealistic goals for him?* Bobby was just the opposite, I doubted he knew the meaning of the word worry, never was on time for anything. He held lengthy conversations with everyone along his paper route, and it took him hours longer than it did Billy to deliver his papers.

Billy was an excellent student, winning a scholarship in his senior year, and according to Bobby's teachers, "He could do as well as his brother if he'd just apply himself."

"I hate it when those stupid teachers tell me how smart Billy was," was Bobby's angry retort.

◆　　◆　　◆

When Jeff was outside with the neighborhood children I found myself constantly peering out to see if he was safe. There were those who enjoyed making fun of him, and when he had had all he could stand of their teasing, he would try to catch his tormentors, only to have them wing away from him laughing.

The pain I felt for him was almost unbearable, and how I wished I could share my feelings with Bill but I had learned this wasn't to be.

11

PRIVATE LESSONS

When fall came Dotty, Tony, Bill and I resumed our Tuesday night skating, and Saturday mornings I took Liz for lessons. Jeff went less and less, saying, "I'd rather stay home and play with Kevin."

If neither Bill nor the older boys were home, they would go to Kevin's house while Liz and I were at the rink.

One Tuesday night as I was untying my skates a young girl in her teens glided over and sat next to me on the bench. "Why don't you let Liz take private lessons? She does so well she could even compete. I've watched her on Saturday mornings, and she's learned all she can from group lessons."

"What do you mean compete?" I asked.

"She would learn to jump, spin and do footwork. Then what she masters will be set to music, and she will skate in front of judges against other girls her age.

"I'll have the think about that," I said hesitantly thinking, "How interesting."

"I wouldn't get involved in competition if I were you," came a voice from the next bench.

I turned to see a woman sitting there with a girl a few years older than Liz dressed in a skating outfit.

"Its expensive and brings nothing but aggravation," she went on.

As I listened I thought *Sounds like sour grapes, otherwise why is her daughter still skating?*

I mulled the idea over in my mind for several weeks, thinking *it might be just the thing to get Liz involved in on her own.* One of my biggest concerns was what would happen to her when we finally lost Jeff. She had always been so close to him. This would keep her busy.

So I approached Carl Henderson, the pro at Bayshore, "Someone suggested starting Liz with private lessons. Do you think she is too young?"

"She is quite young, but if you would like I could give her a couple lessons and see if she is ready?"

◆   ◆   ◆

Liz would take her lessons while her brothers were in school, and from the start I felt the discipline she would learn couldn't hurt her either.

She had been skating several months when Carl suggested, "I think this would be a good time to have her join the skating club. Right after the holidays we start work on our annual show. I want her to be a part of it, but she can not unless she is a member. They meet every Sunday morning here at the rink."

◆   ◆   ◆

I sat and watched the many members rehearsing, ranging in ages from four to forty plus. Those who placed in the top three positions in the previous National Championships were entitled to skate a specialty number.

Always short boys, the racing team, of which Billy was now a member, was asked to fill in. Liz was to skate just one number, one that ended in a giant wheel. The four tallest skaters stood linked together in the center of the rink, two facing in one direction, two in the other, forming the axis. Slowly they began to turn as one by one the rest of the skaters joined on at each end, tallest to the shortest. As they latched on the speed increased till the wheel was revolving very rapidly at the ends. It was going its fastest when Liz's turn came.

The first time she was part of it, I sat with my heart pounding, Two veteran skating mothers sitting nearby did nothing to alleviate my fears. "She shouldn't be out there, she is too tiny. She is going to get hurt," I heard one say to the other just loud enough for me to hear.

I pretended not to. *I'm sure Carl knows what he is doing. He knows what she's capable of,* I reassured myself silently.

The first night of the show Liz received as big a hand as some of the skaters with specialties when she hooked on to her end of the wheel. Looking at the face of one of the <u>concerned</u> mothers I knew she was furious. I'd gotten my first taste of competitive jealously.

12

A NEW WORLD

Liz passed her test, her show performance had been her audition for competition and Carl announced at her next lesson, "We are going to get you ready for AOWs. There is only two weeks, so you are going to have to work very hard." To me he added, "Can you get her here every-day for at least an hour?"

"Sure, we will come while the boys are in school. But what is AOWs?"

"Bayshore rink is a member of the America On Wheels chain, and this competition is held during Easter week in Elizabeth, New Jersey, where the main office is located. It is for skaters from rinks belonging to this chain and insures them money towards Nationals to he held late this summer. It is not necessary to place, just to participate."

In the next two weeks Liz had to learn a minute and a half routine. She couldn't spin yet but did a variety of single jumps (one revolution in the air), footwork and connecting moves all set to a medley of juvenile songs.

There was no thought of Liz going to Nationals at that time, but Carl felt is was a good chance to find out how she performed as a competitor before judges.

Many of the skaters traveled to Jersey the night before they were to compete and stayed in a nearby motel. "It is a ridiculous waste of money," complained Bill. So we left for Jersey early in the morning of the competition.

The night before Bill had taken Liz's skates apart, cleaned the bearings in the wheels and when he finished I polished the boots till they shown. For days I had been working on a special outfit, body of royal blue velvet, white sequin flowers sown, one at the waist and one on one shoulder, a string of matching sequins connecting them and chiffon sleeves of the same shade of blue.

Her dress was hanging in a plastic bag, everything else, hose, hair-brush, hair spray and ribbons to match her outfit were in a small suit-case.

When we arrived at the rink Jeff and Liz were eager to be out of the car even though the rink had not opened its doors yet. I began to feel nervous, wondering what the day would bring.

The first events of the day, figures, began at seven in the morning. Since Liz' division Tiny Tots, was not required to skate them, she wandered around making friends with the other competitors'

All skaters had to be dressed and ready to skate an hour before they were scheduled to compete, in case events progressed quicker than expected.

In a room throbbing with tension, mothers were fussing over many little girls donning their competition attire. I watched as more than one small skater engaged in a verbal battle with an over-anxious parent, thinking, *This is not going to happen to us.*

I helped Liz into her outfit and combed her long blonde hair, parting it in the middle and tying each side in a ponytail with the blue chiffon ribbons. My stomach muscles felt tight as I laced up her skates. She was so little, did not seem nervous, eager to go out and skate her routine. I sent her to Carl and returned to where Jeff and Bill waited. When the time of her event neared all the little girls were sent out on the skating floor for a short warm-up. Then one by one they performed in front of five judges sitting in wooden stands next to the skating surface, pens in hand.

When Liz's turn came she glided onto the floor, stood poised waiting for her music, and I sat frozen in my seat, wondering, *will she remember what she is suppose to do?*

She completed her routine, smiling at the applause as she skated back to Carl. No thought of where the judges might have placed her entered my mind.

When she returned to where we were sitting I could see she was tense. Her father began, "We are going out to lunch now. Take off your skates."

"No," she snapped in an unaccustomed tone, "I don't feel like eating."

Anger glinted in her father's eyes.

"Let her go play awhile. She probably needs to unwind," I said soothingly hoping to avoid any scenes like the ones I had witnessed earlier in the dressing room.

This was her way of reacting to the pressure of competition I learned as she entered more. The tension came after it was over.

When the awards were announced at the end of the day she had won a bronze medal for third place. I was happy for her, almost forgetting for the moment the sadness and apprehension I felt for Jeff most of my waking hours.

13

CHICAGO

On our arrival home as we unloaded the car Bill announced, "I am not driving all the way back there on Friday for some boring dinner. If you two want to go you will have to find someone to take you."

The disappointment in Liz's eyes vanished when I assured her, "We will find someone who has room for us."

I promised myself then I'd do what I could to make her life happy. The effects of Jeff's illness and probable early death were bad enough, and the possibility of her being a carrier was another thing to be dealt with. If skating helped her cope, then she would skate as long as she wanted to, I vowed.

I made her a lavender dress with a white eyelet panel in front for the dinner-dance, and she looked like a little princess with her hair piled high on her head, crowned with a rhinestone tiara.

She was thrilled with the magnitude of the dining room, the dance floor, the live band and almost everybody dressed in formal attire. Many of the little girls in long evening gowns.

"Oh, Mom, look at this fancy bathroom," she squealed when she saw the powder room, constantly disappearing after that, going back for just one more look.

When the announcement was made that the presentation of awards was next I asked one of the older girls, "Would you go see if Liz is in the ladies room again?"

Before she returned a voice behind me inquired, "Does this little girl belong to you?"

Turning, I saw one of the waitresses standing, a grin on her face holding Liz's hand.

"Yes, what did she do?"

"She came into the kitchen and asked if she could help with the dishes."

When the awards were presented, Liz came back with her first bronze medal clutched tightly in her hand. "Mom, how come some of the others got flowers?"

"The girls who came in first got them," I explained.

"I wish I had come in first." She added wistfully.

She soon forgot about the flowers as she leapt up to take part in a game of "Simon Says."

◆   ◆   ◆

On Monday it was back to Bayshore to prepare for the next competition, the state championships. Carl felt she had done well enough at AOWs to skate that one too. The contest would be at our rink so there was no traveling expenses. The only difference, just skaters from New York could participate.

Once again she came in third.

Now a decision had to be made. She was eligible to go to Nationals. Carl urged me to take her, "Just the experience would be priceless, even though her chances of placing are almost nil."

But the championships were to be held in Chicago, and even though some of her expenses would be paid I doubted Bill would agree to go. As expected his reply was, "No way."

But as the deadline for the applications neared the excitement at the rink grew, and Liz caught the fever.

"Daddy, please can't we go?" she pleaded.

Knowing how hard it was for him to refuse her, I added, "Why couldn't Liz and I go? It wouldn't be as expensive that way."

It was finally decided the two of us would go with Carl, Diane and her mother, and Diane's dance partner. Bill would take a week vacation to be home with the boys. I prepared and froze enough meals for the week. I was scared about leaving but was soon caught up in the plans for the trip and pushed any doubts to the back of my mind.

Carl, Mrs. Falco and I were to take turns driving. I'd never driven anyone else's car or driven more than a half-hours distance from home and was extremely nervous.

It took nineteen hours to get to Chicago, and since Liz was violently car sick from Pennsylvania on I did not have to take a turn at the wheel.

We shared a room with Diane and her mother at the hotel where all the skaters were staying, and spent the first day getting acquainted with our surroundings and planning the next day's activities.

The rink was much larger than Bayshore, with American flags draped everywhere and an aura of excitement surpassing anything we had experienced before. Families from almost every state had traveled by plane, car or trailer to participate. Boys and girls carrying skates and garment bags streamed steadily in and out of the rink as the competition progressed. Liz drank in everything like a thirsty puppy, running up to girls she had never seen before, delighting them with comments like, "Good luck, oh what a pretty dress."

The day of her event my stomach was again in knots. *Would she be upset when she didn't win anything?*

She skated her routine the best I had ever seen, and Carl again was pleased, "She could have placed or possibly won if she had had her spins."

Hearing the many compliments made me feel it had been worth all the aggravation.

She placed fifth and did not seem disappointed.

We spent the next few days wandering around Chicago, sitting in the hotel with the other skaters and their families or going to the rink to watch those still competing.

The night before our departure for a home a large formal dinner-dance was held in the ballroom of one of the big hotels. Liz's longing eyes said, "I wish it was me," when the trophies were presented to the winners. I thought, *this might give her the incentive to work harder.*

During the last night Carl completely exhausted by now became ill, and when the time came to start home there were just the three of us. Diane and her mother had gone to meet Diane's father and were planning to tour some of the country before heading home. Carl managed to get us to the outskirts of Chicago and then slept while I took over the wheel. We were three-quarters of the way back before he felt up to driving and on my arrival home I felt like a new person, full of new found confidence, happy to see my family, but tired.

Foolishly I had not called Bill till two days after our arrival in Chicago, thinking it the economical thing to do to wait till Liz skated and I had some real news. At the time Bill had not seemed upset. In fact, a few days after our arrival I opened the door to a knock and found a delivery boy standing there with flowers. I was stunned, never had Bill forgotten birthdays or anniversaries, but to send flowers when there was no special occasion was unheard of.

◆   ◆   ◆

After my return things seemed better until Bill sensed my new confidence, which angered him. He began constantly reminding me that I had not called immediately.

14

THE WEDDING

The remainder of the summer was spent on trips to Fire Island, splashing in the larger pool I had bought to replace the small wading pool, and sleeping out in the tent. A trip to the rink each morning for Liz to practice was added. She did not mind despite the hot muggy weather knowing the pool was waiting.

Another trip to the farm in Salem was included in our itinerary, and this time we took our dog Penny, spending most of the week at the farm because Bill had offered to do some work for Mr. Cummings.

A couple of days after our arrival as I was shampooing my hair a strange and pungent odor drifted through the window.

"Where is Penny:" I asked, afraid I already knew the answer.

"Outside," was Bill's reply, "Why?"

"I think she met up with what she thought was a friendly black cat. But I bet it has a white stripe down its back."

"Ugh! What is that awful smell?" inquired Billy as he came down the stairs.

By then we were all outside watching Penny shake herself violently. We tried washing her, but the smell lingered, and the next day Bill drove into town to buy some strong soap. Then in a nearby brook we scrubbed her over and over. By the time we returned home just a faint odor lingered to remind us of Penny's encounter with the skunk.

◆   ◆   ◆

Before summer's end there was a bridal-shower-barbecue in Cummings' spacious back yard for Kris, the girl Jay was to marry. Liz was asked to be their flower girl. After two years of college Jay enlisted in the army and was stationed in Washington, DC where the wedding was to take place, the half-way point between Jay's family and friends and Kris's.

Bill of course balked at the trip. "We have to go," I protested, "You and Floyd have been such good friends. It won't be that expensive."

"We'll see," was his gruff answer.

◆   ◆   ◆

September arrived and Liz began school, but there was no shyness to overcome, no fears to battle. She was a self-assured young lady, much of which I credited to her skating. Since she attended kindergarten in the mornings, we returned to the same schedule we'd had in the spring, and while she was in school I worked on he dress for Jay's wedding, a floor length yellow lace gown, with matching satin sash. Bill had grudgingly agreed to make the trip to Washington.

On our arrival we had time before the ceremony to do some sightseeing. Till then I had not noticed any real change in Jeff, but now I saw how quickly he tired, how his walking had become more difficult. Liz was thrilled to be part of the wedding, she still worshipped Jay, had always said she would marry him when she got old enough, but at five being his flower girl was as exciting as being his bride.

Jeff's apparent decline was the only thing to mar an otherwise enjoyable weekend.

◆   ◆   ◆

Between school and skating there wasn't much time to brood over Jeff, but I couldn't deny what I had seen. I got up early each morning, preparing everyone's breakfast, sent the children off to school, and Bill to work. Since school for Liz only lasted a few hours I quickly made the beds, vacuumed, did the laundry and began preparations for supper. At noontime when Liz's bus brought her home we had lunch, then went to the rink for practice. We would be back home with supper on the table when Bill returned. The first competition of the new season was held the last weekend in November, in Worchester, Mass., and was to be the first of many first place trophies for Liz. She skated so well that day that one of the more knowledgeable mothers sitting in the stands near us remarked, "I wondered if Liz was just having an unusually lucky day at Nationals. wasn't sure she could do it again. But today she could have beaten anyone."

As thrilled as I was by Liz's performance and the words of praise, I could not shake the feeling of sadness I felt watching Jeff struggle to keep up with the other children, just as he arrived where they had been they were off again.

Surprisingly, Bill had agreed we should all go to the competition, another weekend away, and although he seemed to enjoy watching Liz skate, he crabbed about everything connected with it.

"Staying in a motel is expensive," he complained, even though at that point it was no strain on our budget. I loved it. "This is my idea of a vacation. No cooking, no dishes to wash,

"Who likes sitting around talking about skating? How boring," was his answer.

There were things about this world of competition I did not like, the pushing, punitive parents who wanted trophies for the time and money invested, not caring what kind of person their child was becoming, skaters with fear-filled faces, eyes searching for parents looking for understanding when they fell or missed a jump.

But for me the positive outweighed the negative. Skating was accomplishing just what I had hoped it would, Liz had found a life separate from her beloved brother. As young as she was I could see how much time she devoted to him. She needed something to fall back on when the time came when he was no longer around.

There were a few other competitions that winter, and Liz brought home first place trophies from each. I was glad it was going so well for her but wished there were more for Jeff, something that would give him a chance to actively participate with normal youngsters.

"If I could find an indoor swimming pool where he could swim during the school year, it might be just the thing." I mused out loud, thinking of his love for the water.

"You are crazy! What happens if he can't swim?" Bill muttered.

"He's no different than anyone else. How is he going to know if he doesn't try?" was my reply.

"Suppose he does learn. Then when he can not swim anymore, how is he going to feel?"

"That is stupid. You might as well say why bother to learn to walk. I think it is worth the risk. He can even take lessons if he wants," I shot back defiantly.

"Now I know you have lost your mind. Do not include me in your ridiculous scheme." And stormed out of the room.

When I first thought about Jeff's swimming I had hoped Bill would help with some of the driving, the school psychologist constantly told me Jeff needed more male companionship, but his father's last remark squashed that idea. If he only knew what he was missing by keeping his distance from his son.

My participation in Jeff's school activities, especially field trips, made me aware of how others felt about Jeff, how special he was to everyone. The teachers especially loved him. There was a loving trust he had in everything and everyone. Never did he question why he had this condition. "I'd rather be like this than blind," he declared on more than one occasion.

I finally found a school with a pool and thanks to Mr. Wexler, Director of Health and Physical Education, he was welcome to swim every Friday evening after supper.

That first trip was scary. *Suppose Bill was right? Am I doing the right thing?* My old insecurities flooding back.

I watched him that first time, arms swinging walk slowly to the edge of the pool, then with extreme effort, lower himself into the water.

Once in, he was free of all restrictions, normal, well almost. I felt uneasy as his first lesson began, until I saw he could do everything as well and in some instances better than the others in the group.

As the months passed I wished Bill could share in the pride and happiness I gleaned watching Jeff swim. Then one night after our weekly sojourn Liz pleaded, "Mom, why can't I swim too?"

"I'm sorry but this is Jeff's thing. You have your skating." I knew she would excel and take some of the pleasure out of it for him.

"Why can't Liz swim too?" demanded Bill as we were preparing for bed that night, "I heard her asking."

"Jeff needs this. It's the first time he has been able to compete with normal children and by the way, doing better than a lot of them. I will not take the chance it will be spoiled."

"You think you have all the answers, don't you? He snarled as he stormed out of the room.

15

A FALL

Show time at the roller rink was approaching, and now the whole family was involved, even Jeff. Although he dressed as a gypsy for the big wheel only as a background extra it made him feel a part of things, but it meant I had to produce eight costumes, without patterns, copying models and a special outfit for Liz's solo number. I relished the challenge, hadn't I always created Halloween costumes without patterns?

She had not placed in the top three at Nationals; the usual criterion for being awarded such a number, and I wondered if it was wise giving her one before she had earned it? But I said nothing.

Practice for the show was held Friday and Saturday nights following the public session. It was close to midnight by the time the rink was cleared and rehearsals began. Liz, always a night person, thrived on the late hours. It would be two, sometimes three in the morning before we returned home. Jeff needed his sleep, so most of the time he stayed at home with Dotty and Tony.

Rather than have us at the rink so late at night alone, Bill volunteered to help build props.

Each club member was required to sell a specific number of show tickets, and the more they sold, the more money they earned towards their expenses for nationals. Liz, petite, cute and unaffected by the attention she received because of her skating, made friends with many of those who skated only during regular sessions, both young and old and had no trouble selling more than her share.

"You are no better than any of the other little girls who come to skate, just luckier," I would remind her often. This plus the awareness of Jeff's problems kept her from becoming a "prima donna" like so many of the other competitive skaters.

Bobby was now taking roller dance lessons and was asked to participate in the show. Along with Billy, he was part of the big wheel.

Immediately following the show the competitive skaters again began preparing for AOWs. Liz had won every competition up till then and was more than eager to win this one, she had not forgotten about that bouquet of flowers first place skaters were presented with at the dinner-dance. She worked very hard on her new routine and had mastered her spins nicely.

The day of the meet we left home early in the morning for Jersey. Billy was competing in figures and freestyle. A broken collarbone suffered while racing, and his experience in the show the year before had gotten him interested in the artistic side of skating. I'd spent weeks making a black tux for him and a bright yellow outfit for Liz. After my experiences with the show costumes even the idea of tackling the job of making a tux had lost its formidability.

Billy skater his figures first and because of his strong power of concentration did a beautiful job. For him the freestyle, jumping and spinning were much more difficult. He was now seventeen and six feet tall. I felt a great deal of pride in his efforts, knowing it took a lot of courage to do what seemed easy for his little sister. Instead of resenting her though a special bond grew between them, and during practice they would sometimes have contests to see whom was the first to miss a jump.

During warm-up that day in Jersey, Liz's jumps looked clean (no pulls on the landings) and she was spinning well. There were about eight other girls on the floor, all under six, but some much bigger than Liz. As she was coming out of a spin a girl much taller and heavier came barreling into her, knocking her down. She got up slowly, tears streaming down her face, and painfully skated over to us.

"Are you all right?" I asked anxiously.

"It's my knee," she sobbed. "That stupid girl is suppose to watch out for the spinners."

"Here let me see," looking at the red mark, I thought *It will probable turn into an ugly bruise* rubbing it gently I asked, "Do you think you can skate?"

"I'll try," she said wiping at the tears on her cheeks before heading back to where Carl stood.

I was relieved when she completed her routine but surprised when Carl approached afterwards frowning, "That is the worst I have ever seen her skate. What is wrong with her today?"

I looked at him puzzled; "Didn't you see what happened during warm-ups?"

"No."

"She got knocked down by that big girl in red, and hurt her knee. I was surprised she even made it through her routine. I think she did quite well under the circumstances," I added defensively.

I learned later that his attention had been diverted by the mother of a little girl from our rink who was getting ready to compete against Liz. This mother, a competitive skater herself since she was a teenager, was one of the worst examples of a skating mother, determined to make her daughter a champion no matter what it took. "I know every trick in the book," she bragged at practice one day.

I was satisfied when Liz was awarded third place; with each first pressure had been building. Now we would see how she reacted when she didn't get the first-place trophy. I was really proud of her as she accepted the bronze medal with the same graciousness as she had all the firsts, but I was sorry she didn't get those flowers she had worked so hard for.

16

THE CLIMB BACK

As I sat on the hard bench at the rink in Bayshore watching Liz's next lesson, I thought, *Carl must have given up on her because he seems less intent.* To me it did not matter as long as she was enjoying herself. I was more concerned with Billy, who would find it hard to accept if he did not do well. Liz didn't really understand the meaning of competition; she just loved to skate, especially before an audience, and did not care if she was the "best?"

After the first of the year she attended kindergarten in the afternoon, so practice had to be moved to after school when all the other skaters were there, and we saw more and more of the bad side of this sport. Parents threatening and sometimes even following through with actual beatings, when their children didn't practice or perform the way they felt they should.

I watched appalled. Couldn't they see how lucky they were their children could walk, run, skate? And yes, compete for trophies and medals.

There was constant friction over the use of the record player, some skaters returned the needle to the beginning of their record if they fell, ignoring the line of skaters waiting to play theirs'.

Liz was friendly and vivacious, and most of the older girls tried to "mother" her, but she wanted no part of that. Some were jealous because the older boys preferred her as a partner during session when "Dance Steps" were played.

Liz had no favorites, she liked everyone.

One day during practice when she was trying to help a new skater with a jump another club member in her early teens yelled at her, "Liz, come here! What do you think you are doing?"

"I am helping her with her mapes."

"Look, kid, Nora is a creep. Don't encourage her, we don't want the likes of her joining the club," added Marla sarcastically.

"But she is nice, I like her. You can not tell me who to be friends with!" Liz threw back angrily as she skated back to where Nora waited.

◆   ◆   ◆

Billy was trying to fit freestyle and figure practice in between a job at a local drug store and school, and the day of the championships I was apprehensive. He was nervous to begin with and was under even more pressure skating before a panel of judges. He was in a special class called "Intra", for new skaters over sixteen. There were no competitors opposing him that day so the judges could give him any placement they felt he deserved. In all divisions above Tiny Tots the skaters had to place in the top eight in figures to qualify for freestyle.

Billy's figures were good so we were not concerned with them putting him that low but if the judges decided his freestyle wasn't National material they could give him as low as fourth, preventing him from going any further.

"It would be easier to skate against at least one other person then the judges would have to award me first or second," he complained.

I was extremely tense as he skated his routine, and we waited for the results to be posted, but much to my relief he was given second, which meant he would be skating in Nationals in Cleveland, Ohio.

When it came time for Liz to skate she did much better than she had after the collision during warm-ups at AOWs. Watching her glide gracefully to her music I could block momentarily all the fear and sadness I felt for Jeff. She moved up to second and didn't appear upset by the results.

After receiving her silver medal she headed for the ladies room to change into her regular clothes and a few minutes later marched back, a mixture of anger and fear on her face. "Jody says the judges made a mistake today. She says she should have gotten second, not me. Its not true, is it?"

"Of course not. You skated well and deserved it. Don't pay any attention to her. She is just mad because you beat her this time." I assured her. *Was it possible this had come from the mind of a six-year old?*

Back at Bayshore Carl continued giving Liz lessons, but the pressure was gone, and I was just glad Liz was going to Nationals. I knew then that I would never make the good skating mother many felt I should be. I'd do whatever I could to help Liz, but what she wanted to do with her skating was up to her.

◆　　　◆　　　◆

I loved making practice and competition outfits and could not resist the fabric department in J.C. Penney or the material store in the mall. But there was a stall in the Farmer's Market, directly across from the rink, and in spite of the nauseating smell of fish and cheese, was an endless source of pleasure. Never did I come away with just one piece of fabric. Sol, the owner, could fill almost any request. When Spandex became the favored material for outfits he had a large variety to choose from, and Liz had skating dresses of ever color and design.

◆　　　◆　　　◆

There was no question about going to Cleveland. Liz and Billy would both receive money towards their expenses and it posed no financial hardship for us all to make the trip.

I had bought Jeff a View Master Projector for Christmas hoping when we traveled Bill would take him to visit historical landmarks, since neither enjoyed sitting around the rink or motel listening to skate talk. I figured they could purchase slides of the places they saw, and Jeff could show them on his projector at home. But even if we had not been forced by the racial rioting in Cleveland that summer to remain either at the rink or motel I doubt it would have worked. Deep down I knew Bill would resist any plan of mine.

The rink was bustling with excitement, flags hanging from the rafters, music blaring and skaters nervously pacing, waiting their turn to perform. My main concern still was Billy. At seven-thirty in the morning he did a beautiful job and placed well up near the top in figures, against eighteen other young men, and that afternoon was among the top eight who skated their routines.

One skater from California had such fantastic freestyle he would have knocked Billy out of a chance for a medal if it had not been for Billy's figures. But he held onto third, making both Liz and I proud.

As in the previous year in Chicago Liz was enjoying herself immensely, wandering around the rink making friends with girls from all over the country.

She was scheduled to skate that same evening, and luckily the rink was air conditioned, it was steaming outside. All Liz could think about was doing her program so she could get back to the motel for a swim in the pool she had gazed at longingly each time she passed it.

"No swimming till after you skate," Carl informed his skaters. "The water loosens up the muscles too much.

"Dressed in a bright yellow outfit, black sequins at her throat, her golden hair piled high on her head, she looked so grown up and yet so tiny.

As each of the seventeen girls went on the ice for the warm-ups I felt the tension building in me praying, *Just let her skate well.*

One of the first to take the floor was Jody, the girl who had told Liz the judges had made a mistake at the state competition. She stroked onto the floor looking very self-assured and glided around, jumping and spinning. *Liz has to be at her best to beat her. Jody looks great.* Suddenly she stopped, frozen for a few seconds, and then left the floor tears cascading down her face. A hush came over the rink and then whispered questions tiptoed from one to another.

"What happened?" "What is wrong?"

There was a conference at the judges' stand and then an announcement, "Jody will try again after the last skater."

She had forgotten her routine.

When Liz's turn came, I watched nervously. She appeared calm, and I tried not to think how sure Jody had seemed, but Liz skater better than I had ever seen her skate, jumping and spinning, smiling broadly. Having fun. Her effervescence captivated the crowd, and they applauded long and loudly when she left the floor at the end. She came to us after a few words with Carl, I hugged her, and then she skated off to find her new friends. She had done what she came to do.

We learned later that Jody refused to reskate her routine and words Carl once offered echoed in my mind. Every*thing evens out in the end.*

17

CHAMPION

The score sheets for each event were hung on a wall where everyone crowded around as the Tiny Tots results were posted, and when the judges' decisions were sorted out Liz was the National Champion. I was stunned, everyone from Bayshore at the rink that night went wild, Carl lifted Liz to his shoulders, grinning broadly, and even Bill looked pleased.

On our arrival back at the motel the pool was already closed for the night.

"I wanted to swim, Liz cried in disappointment.

But soon forgot as everyone crowded into our room. Chaos! Pillows flew, beds became trampolines.

◆　　　◆　　　◆

Before leaving for home we attended the dinner-dance and presentation of awards, and Liz was thrilled because she could wear her yellow gown from Jay's wedding. She was awarded a gold medal, hanging from a ribbon of red, white and blue, and a trophy that would be her's for a year. He name would be engraved on it along with all the other Tiny Tots who had won before her. It was large, almost as tall as she was, and when she clutched it to her slim body to carry it to the car her father snatched it growling, "You'll drop it." Tears of resentment filled her eyes, but I managed to calm her, and we returned to the motel to rest before heading home.

◆   ◆   ◆

No sooner were we back then Liz wanted to go to the rink for a figure lesson, something she had been anxious to do for quite some time.

The remainder of the summer flew by, and when school opened Liz went into first grade and was in school for a full day. After school I took her to practice and for lessons. Bobby was working in the skate room and taking dance lessons from Carl's wife Barbara, who was looking for a dance partner for him. Billy was in his last year of high school, talking about college, skating and working in the drug store, and again I wished there was more for Jeff. While watching Liz practice one day an idea began to form, and I could hardly wait to get home to ask Jeff what he thought, "How would you like to learn to play a musical instrument?"

"Could I really? But what?"

"A guitar maybe?"

After a few moments thought he asked expectantly, "When can I start?"

"Let me see what I can find out. Just think, if you learn to play well you could even join a band when you are older." Leaving unspoken, *Since you won't be dancing.*

"Can I go tell Kevin?" he asked excitedly, turning abruptly towards the door bumping into his father.

"Where is he going in such a rush?"

"Just to tell Kevin he is going to take guitar lessons."

"What! Another one of your hair-brained schemes, I suppose," he spat at me.

"I was not wrong about swimming, was I?" I could not resist remarking.

"You are just lucky it worked out," he grumbled as he went into the bathroom slamming the door.

◆　　　◆　　　◆

The next day I began my search for a teacher. <u>Pennysaver</u> a small local paper yielded a few possibilities, and I began calling until I found one that fit our needs, and arrangements were made.

"You can rent a guitar until you are sure the lessons are going to work out," the teacher assured me.

So every Tuesday I left Liz at the rink practicing while I drove Jeff to Brentwood for his lesson, and was surprised at how quickly he learned to read music. His success prompted me to question the psychologist at school about giving Jeff a trial in a regular education class.

"His reading level is not quite up to where it should be. He is not ready for that yet." She discouraged me.

I realize now I should have demanded he be given a chance then but was intimidated by her degrees and apparent infallibility.

For his ninth birthday I bought Jeff a shiny new guitar emblazoned with a rose, and whenever anyone came to visit he scurried to his room to get it, even though it took some coaxing before he would play it for them.

Mrs. Dickensen, his teacher, convinced him to bring it to school to play for the class. He took it proudly and surprised me with the assurance with which he performed. Even though his guitar lessons added another trip to my itinerary I was happy it had turned out so well.

◆　　　◆　　　◆

Show time came at the rink, another AOWs. Would Billy win the championship this year? Liz was at the bottom of the Juvenile division, and we knew there would be no more trophies for her for awhile. But this was Billy's last chance, in the fall he would begin college.

Just as the year before he was the only "Intra" skater in the state championships

Unfortunately, one of the judges, a former competitor herself from our own club felt she had to advise him and approached him after he finished his figures, with his freestyle still to come. "I can't believe how shaky you were. From your ankles down you were steady as a rock but the rest of you was trembling like a leaf."

As I stood listening I thought, *Am I hearing right?* Her next words stunned me even more.

"Why don't you take tranquilizers when you skate?"

"If I can't do it without them, I would rather forget it." He snapped.

As she walked away I realized the full extent of what had just occurred. She had succeeded in making him even more unsure of himself.

"Does that mean she marked me low on my figures?" fear tinged his words. "Why couldn't she wait till after my freestyle?"

The tension was unbearable. Would he "blow" his routine and his chance to go to Nationals? Had she done it deliberately? She did have a son who skated. I felt ill as we waited.

His routine went smoothly, no falls and combined with his high figure marks, he was awarded second. Which meant he would be competing in Nationals later that summer.

18

AND THE RAINS CAME

As the weather warmed that spring I began thinking about investing in a larger swimming pool since Jeff had mastered the skills needed to pass the advanced beginner test at Connequot, and the pool we had wasn't big enough to swim in. I searched the papers for advertisements and sales, considering a four foot deep, round pool, an oval one with an expandable section under which you could dig deep enough to make it possible even to dive. Then one day I passed a place that sold do-it-yourself pools, and for a couple hundred dollars more we could install one in the ground. When I mentioned it to Bill he was anything but receptive. "A thousand dollars! Are you crazy? Where do you think you'll find that kind of money?"

"Take out a home improvement loan. With an inground pool Jeff could swim in the shallow end and the others in the deep. We certainly have enough room for it." It wasn't till years later I realized the in ground pool made things a lot easier. An above the ground pool would have become impossible to get Jeff in as his condition deteriorated. Everyone, the children, Dotty, Tony and I began emphasizing how good it would be for Jeff, till Bill finally caught our enthusiasm and agreed to apply for a loan of $2000, enough to cover the cost of the pool, fencing and landscaping. The only one not excited over it was Billy.

"The kids at school think it is awful you are thinking of installing a pool when you should be worrying about helping me with college." He said with a look of indignation on his face.

Angrily I snapped at him, "You are not the only one to be considered. Didn't you explain to your friends why we are doing it? And besides, it is none of their business how we spend our money."

He had turned down a PTA scholarship because he did not want to go to school in New York; Georgetown, one of the most expensive, was his choice. His father and I finally agreed to sign up for a tuition plan and Billy applied for a student loan.

"You are going to have to work part-time if you need more money, I warned.

We went ahead with plans for the pool. We had gotten the loan and purchased the pool from a fellow worker of Bill's who ran a pool business on the side.

I phoned the building department to inquire about what permits we needed. It was a few days before Memorial Day and I figured it would be a good weekend to begin installing it. I was told, "Come down with a diagram of you proposed pool, and you will have your permit."

But much to my dismay when I presented the plans to them I was told, "You have to put the pool in your back yard. Where it is shown on the diagram, it is on the side. Because you are on a corner your side is considered part of you front yard.

"But that is impossible, the cesspool and overflow are in the back. We are putting it to the rear of that side piece of property. How can you say that is the front yard?" my voice shook with disbelief and disappointment.

"I'm sorry, you will have to apply for a variance then. The town board has to approve it."

Close to tears, I asked, "How long will that take?"

He glanced at the calendar on the wall behind him, "Next board meeting is the fifteenth of June." "But summer will be half over by then."

"Sorry."

◆   ◆   ◆

I left there feeling devastated, picturing the disappointed faces when they heard, and as I neared house my heart sank even lower, sitting in the middle of the yard, big and yellow was the backhoe, a large machine for digging trenches, borrowed from the lighting company. And there it remained, a painful reminder the entire weekend.

I knew the town board could refuse to grant us a variance, so hoping to improve our chances I wrote a letter to the town supervisor explaining Jeff's situation and how important the pool was to him.

On the fifteenth, sitting listening to other appeals and hearing those opposed my heart raced. Would the neighbor who had called the police on Jeff show up and object just for spite? She had been notified along with the other neighbors of our plans.

Her daughter had been teasing Jeff about his funny walk one afternoon when Liz and I were at the rink, Jeff had gotten angry, and when she ran away laughing, because he was unable to catch her he picked up a small pebble and hurled it in her direction hitting their garage door.

Bobby told us what had happened when we returned home from the rink. "I was having a sandwich, heard a commotion outside, and when I went out a police car was pulling up out front. Jeff was so scared he hid behind me. The cop himself was embarrassed when he realized whom the neighbor had called to complain about, and told me just to watch him closer, then left in a big hurry.

Luckily, my fears proved groundless, no one objected, the variance was ours.

Bill again made arrangements to borrow the backhoe, and we watched wide-eyed as the hole grew; sixteen foot wide by thirty-two foot long, four foot deep at one end to eight foot at the other. Once the hole was dug it had to be shaped to exact specifications with shovels.

Billy wasn't expected to help with any of the work; he would soon leave for Georgetown. Instead Bobby had to take his place as his father's helper, which he resented immensely.

When his father yelled, which was often, I would plead with Bobby, "Just stick it out till the pool is finished. You will be glad you did. Believe me, it will be well worth it."

Bobby shoveled, sweated and steamed, and between him and his father they had the hole shaped, ready for the sides and liner within a few days. When they reached that point we went to bed filled with happy anticipation, like children on Christmas Eve, but the next morning we were as heartsick as those children would have been if Santa had not come. The sky was gray, drizzle filled the air turning into a torrential downpour. It rained for the remainder of Bill's vacation, almost a week and a half, turning the carefully contoured hole into a giant mud-filled crater, the meticulously sculptured sides sliding to the bottom.

When it finally stopped, and the water drained off they had to spend another weekend reshaping it, then the steel walls were put in place, fastened, the liner lowered in, and the steel coping attached over the edges of both. Using an extra wide hose he'd borrowed from his uncle, Bill began filling the pool, but when I saw the liner as not lying flat in the deep end, I warned, "You better not add more water till you straighten out the liner."

I knew he resented any suggestions from me, but past experience had taught me once the water was in there was no way to straighten out the liner.

"It will impossible," I pleaded.

"Don't tell me, the water will flatten it out. I know what I am doing," he scoffed.

I knew I had to do something, and fast, this involved thousands of gallons of water, so I quickly went into the house, called Ed, the man from whom we'd bought the pool and explained the situation.

"Is he crazy? He will have to empty all the water out and start over."

"I know, but he will not listen to me. Could you please just happen to stop by to see how things are progressing? Do not let on I called you though. Please."

"I will be right over."

I busied myself in the house, not wanting to be out there when Ed arrived, and when I heard the truck door slam a few minutes later I stealthily peeked from behind the dining room curtains.

Bill, all smiles, almost obeisant, was emptying out the water.

19

GEORGETOWN

While we concentrated on our plans for the pool, Billy was preparing for Nationals which was to be held in Levittown late in July, getting ready for graduation and working in the drug store.

On graduation day as I watched Billy and his classmates receive their diplomas I felt that old twinge of sadness. Would Jeff be here for his?"

◆   ◆   ◆

With the installation of the pool dominating our lives Nationals seemed to arrive very quickly. Billy wanted to end his skating career with a gold medal, and I prayed his hard work would pay off.

It seemed strange not having Liz competing too. But she insisted on going to watch her brother.

I felt my stomach muscles tighten when it came time for him to do his routine, praying nothing would go wrong. He had a good lead in figures and skated his freestyle well, no misses, no falls. There were some anxious moments waiting for the scores to be posted, but when the results were tallied his dream had come true. He, like his sister was a National Champion.

Following Nationals he spent most of his free time driving to Jersey to see Ginny, a girl he had met at one of the competitions earlier in the year. He had had a few girl friends before but none as friendly and as at ease with us as she was when he brought her to visit.

As the time for his departure for Georgetown drew near he began having doubts, gone was the happy anticipation he had had when we had made the financial arrangements, but Ginny and I convinced him he should go. She went with us when we drove him to Washington, D.C. and it wasn't easy to say good-bye when we left to return home. As I glimpsed the lonely figure waving from the cold, stark dorm window I prayed he would stick it out.

The first few months were difficult for both of us. There were daily phone calls from school, he was depressed, homesick, sorry he had gone.

It scared me to hear how unhappy he was. I wanted to refuse his calls but was too apprehensive. I had heard tales of suicides by students in their first few months away from home and feared what he might do.

He was afraid Ginny would find someone else, and I tried to reassure him, "If she is the right one, things will work out."

The collect calls pushed the phone bill higher and higher. By the middle of November his letters were filled with hate for Georgetown. Nothing was the way he had expected it to be, most of the students were from wealthy families who could send money whenever it was asked for. My budget was feeling the strain between the tuition payments and the high phone bills, and I felt it was time he worked things out for himself.

"Try and find a part-time job. It will give you more money and less time to brood," I suggested, and finally put my foot down. "No more collect calls unless it is an emergency."

Next he wanted his car, which was sitting in the yard in need of a great deal of work, and neither his father nor I felt it was worth putting money into. Letter after letter came, first begging, then demanding that we have the necessary repairs done. I wrote, trying to reason with him, but in return he accused me of having no compassion.

I knew the main reason for wanting the car was so he could drive to Jersey to see Ginny, but he also had a scheme for making money.

"I could run a taxi service for other students that want to come east too."

"A bad accident with a bunch in your car, and we could lose everything. You must be crazy."

He felt it was worth the risk; wasn't concerned about us. Never did he ask how Jeff was doing, and I began to feel he was like his father, either could not or would not face up to what was happening to his brother.

◆   ◆   ◆

About a month after Billy left for Georgetown proficiency tests were scheduled at the rink, and both Liz and Bobby were to take dance tests. The tests began early Sunday morning, running into club time. The atmosphere was much like that of a competition, a panel of judges were to decide if the skaters had mastered the dances. To Liz it was a lark, she loved to dance.

Bobby, though, was unusually withdrawn that morning. I knew part of it was nervousness since it was his first appearance before judges, but sensed there was more.

Each category or test level was given a short warm-up, and just before Bobby's I asked, "What is wrong? You are awfully quiet."

"Mom, I just feel terrible. It just is not fair," he blurted out. "Jeff misses out on so much. At first he liked to skate too, and now he does not even come to the rink anymore." Unshed tears glistened in his eyes.

My own eyes began to sting but I tried to console him, "Jeff would feel bad if you didn't do things because of him. He accepts his limitations without complaining, don't make him feel bad. Go out there and do your best."

For the first time I realized how much Jeff's condition was affecting his brother.

◆   ◆   ◆

Meanwhile Jeff was showing signs that Muscular Dystrophy was stealthily robbing him of his strength. He fell more, getting up was more difficult and he tired more easily. As soon as the weather turned cool, and he was swimming only once a week I could see an even more rapid decline. Once he lost ground, it would never be regained.

Bill was working overtime almost every day and weekends, and I found I preferred being alone with the children,. Now that Liz was no longer bringing home trophies her father complained constantly, "Skating is a waste of money. You're always up at the damn rink."

"Its good for both of us. I worry less about Jeff if I'm not with him all the time, and Liz needs some time away from him too." She was spending whatever free time she had at school, lunchtime and recess in his classroom helping his teacher.

Bill tried to dominate Bobby as he had Billy. "I want the grass cut, the weeding and trimming done by tomorrow."

"But I am suppose to go to Kathy's before I go to work."

"You get that done first." The threat of a beating with the belt didn't faze Bobby. From the time he was small if he got hit by his father he refused to cry; which angered Bill even more. But with each incident resentment grew. Bobby worked at the roller rink in the skate room and was everybody's friend, especially the "bad element" that frequented the rink on weekends. Would he do something stupid just to spite his father? It was like he was walking a tightrope, which way would he fall?

◆   ◆   ◆

Every summer the National champions were asked to put on an exhibition at Jones Beach. The cement surface was not easy to skate on, an old worn-out set of wheels had to be used because they would be useless afterwards, but it had been a dream of Liz's to be part of that show since she had witnessed one when she first started skating. It meant more to her than a specialty number in the show at the rink, but the little girl whose mother had bragged about knowing all the tricks was asked instead. Liz cried bitterly, one of the few times she shed tears over skating.

Then there was a time when she overheard one of the mothers say, "She is not that good," and Liz remarked, "What's so great about being a champion? People were nicer to me before."

But most of the time she was happy to be skating, and if something did upset her at home or school it was a panacea. A good example was the day she came home from school very disturbed over an incident on the bus. "Those Cleary kids said they are glad Jeff is going to die. How can they talk like that when they put on carnivals to raise money for kids with MD?"

Once at the rink she never left the skating surface, and I wished Bill could see how much skating was a benefit to her.

20

A HOSPITAL STAY

Although Kevin still came over to see Jeff often I began to doubt his friendship. He belittled Jeff's ability to swim lap after lap, as many as thirty times from one end of the pool to the other. Jeff swam slowly with an uncanny buoyancy using an unconventional style all his own, depending almost entirely on his arms, hardly moving his legs.

"Anyone can do that," bragged Kevin.

With obvious irritation in my voice I directed, "You get in there and swim like he does without using your legs and then tell me it's so easy."

Witnessing this Bobby asked me angrily, "Why does Jeff bother with him? He doesn't care about Jeff, he just comes to use the pool."

"I know, but that's not important. Jeff needs <u>someone</u>. If they come because of the pool at least he has company."

Jeff had lost his friends the Jones boys when they'd moved back to the city."

He'd spent a night at the home of one of the boys from the special class once, but the boy's mother had hovered over Jeff so much, afraid he'd get hurt, he hadn't wanted to go back.

Again I was thankful for Liz's skating. I didn't have to watch the ever increasing loneliness caused by Jeff's attendance in special class. The youngsters he should have been with gradually forgot about his very existence, the neighborhood children not including him in their parties, and he'd sit in the driveway watching them romping and playing without him.

◆   ◆   ◆

When reading a magazine one day I found an ad for a bubble to cover the swimming pool, making it possible to swim long after the weather had turned chilly. When I showed it to Bill he just glanced at it, shrugged his shoulders and walked away. It would be perfect for Jeff. I often told him he should have been born a fish since he was the happiest in the water.

Between Christmas and the opening of school following the New Year, there was no place for Jeff to swim. He became quiet and withdrawn, and when I questioned if there was something bothering him he said, "My legs hurt."

And again the idea of the bubble surfaced in my mind. It might be the answer. As soon he resumed his weekly swimming the change was evident. He scurried around the house, his old self again. More and more I was determined to find a way he could swim longer. It wasn't a cure but a way of keeping him feeling fit and just maybe even slowing the progress of the disease.

During a visit to the MD clinic with my nephew. my sister Jo questioned the doctor as to why they didn't recommend swimming for these children. "It's better not to start them on something they'll eventually be unable to continue. It's even harder for them to accept when they can't do it anymore," was the answer. One I couldn't and wouldn't accept.

A mother who'd been through an experience with a dying child told me. "Some doctors feel the outcome will be the same no matter what the parents do, so they encourage them to do what they feel is good for the child. Then when death comes there will be less guilt to be dealt with."

Why, I wondered, did other doctors deny that even though things were supposed to be hopeless that the will to live could change the outcome? Even Dr. Bernhardt scolded me when I appeared optimistic about Jeff's progress. "You're not facing reality," he'd accuse. He was so wrong.

I was ever aware of the probability of Jeff's death but tried to make the most of the time we had. His birthdays were painful, one less year remaining, was all I could think as we celebrated in the same way we did for Liz and his brothers. But when I was alone the tears fell.

I had realized my nephew Edward was also a victim of this dread disease long before my sister was aware anything was wrong, seeing the same symptoms I'd overlooked or minimized in Jeff. But I kept it to myself, she would know soon enough.

◆　　　◆　　　◆

When the time came for Jeff's annual re-evaluation at the clinic the doctor was pleased with the fact that the tendons in the back of his ankles which normally tightened up in dystrophic patients were still fairly loose.

"I want you to take Jeff to Good Samaritan Hospital for a blood test. Maybe a wrong diagnosis was made." My hopes soared as we entered the hospital a few days later and for several days after as we waited for the results I tried to keep my imagination in check. *Oh, let it be a big mistake,* I prayed. There was no doubt something was wrong but at least let it not be fatal.

But the call came, and my spirits plunged. There had been no mistake, the blood test confirmed it, but for some reason the progress of the disease was moving much slower than usual. I was convinced it was the swimming and even more positive he'd walk much longer than they'd predicted, but fate stepped in.

I'd taken Liz for a ballet lesson one afternoon late in May and on our arrival home was greeted by Dotty, "There has been a slight accident. Jeff's scratched up a little but nothing serious."

One look at Jeff and nausea swept over me. He was deathly pale, front tooth broken, knees badly scraped and obviously in shock.

"My God, what happened?" I almost screamed at her.

"Kevin and Jeff were walking on the dead-end, a neighbor backed out of her driveway and didn't see them. Kevin was able to run out of the way, but Jeff couldn't, and the car knocked him down. But he's all right."

On the verge of hysteria I ran into the house and called Dr. Bernhardt.

"Bring him to my office at once!"

Between Dotty and I, we half dragged, half carried him into the van and sped to the doctor's office. Once inside he examined him thoroughly. "I'm afraid his leg might be broken. I'm calling an ambulance to take him to Southside. How did you ever get him here? he asked not really expecting an answer. The ambulance arrived, and one of the attendants applied a balloon-like splint to Jeff's right leg before placing him on a stretcher and carrying him to the waiting ambulance.

"We'll turn on the siren for you," offered the driver hoping to divert Jeff's attention but only causing him more discomfort instead. With the siren screaming we rode from East Islip, through Islip to Bayshore, while I held on tightly praying he wasn't hurt too badly.

On our arrival at Southside, around three in the afternoon Jeff was placed on a gurney in the hallway next to the emergency room to wait his turn to be x-rayed. I left Dotty behind to call the lighting company, and have Bill pick her and the van up on his way home from work. No thought of calling him had entered my mind till then. When he arrived at the hospital the x-rays had been taken and I was waiting for the results.

It wasn't until seven that evening that we were finally told, "The car passed completely over his right leg. The pubic bone, a small curved bone that joins the leg to the torso is fractured. Because of its location we can't put him in a cast. We're keeping him overnight for observation to make sure there are no internal injuries. With these words tears welled up in Jeff's eyes for the first time. Fighting them back he asked, "Do I have to stay?"

"I'm afraid so. We'll go home and get your pjs and toothbrush. We'll be back by the time you're settled in your room. It'll be all right," I tried to reassure him.

Dotty and Tony offered to stay with the others till we got back from taking him his things. When we returned they went home, and we tried to relax by watching a movie on TV, and in an attempt at humor to lighten the mood that had settled over us and referring to the constant barking of Penny and another neighborhood dog I said, "The natives are restless tonight."

No sooner were the words out of my mouth than the alarm Bill had rigged up in the garage, blatantly ripped through the night air. It had been installed to warn us if anyone got in the pool area, a precaution against a possible drowning accident.

Bobby grabbed the floor mop, hurtled out the door with his father in hot pursuit, and they saw someone dive over the back pool fence. By the time Bobby reached the spot whoever it was made a clean get-away on a bicycle left on the other side.

With screens, Bill had turned the garage into a porch-like room where we spent much of our time during the summer, and we decided attempted robbery must have been the reason for the break-in.

A few minutes later Nick, a friend of Bill's, stopped by to inquire about Jeff and was astounded by our most recent adventure. "This place is crazy! Wasn't Jeff's accident enough excitement enough for one day?"

21

A QUESTION

The next two weeks were spent running to the hospital to visit Jeff. He was overjoyed to see us, but a hint of tears appeared in his eyes when visiting hours were over. What had begun as an overnight stay stretched into two long weeks.

He questioned us daily when he could come home, and his father concerned with what it was costing was impatient to oblige. Because of my fear that he might not walk again I wanted him to stay as long as the doctors felt it necessary. I knew how difficult it had been for both Dotty and I to get him into the van, how would I be able to manage on my own?

Memories of my brother flooded back. Thirty years earlier doctors had diagnosed him with what they called "creeping paralysis", more than likely Muscular Dystrophy, but back then no one had even given it a name. On his way to school one morning he slipped on some loose gravel, fell breaking his leg, and when it healed it was shorter than the other one. In all probability the tightening of the tendon in back of his foot, something common in dystrophy, had been more rapid in the injured leg. When the doctors attempted to "stretch his spine" he died during the operation. I'd been advised not to allow a dentist to even administer gas. This made me wonder if the anesthesia had stopped my brother's heart?

Except for when it came time for us to leave Jeff seemed to be enjoying himself. He had made a couple of friends, and we were told of races in the halls in the wheelchairs.

Bill's concern over the expense and mine over what the results of this stay would mean caused several heated arguments. "Don't you want him to come home?" accused Bill.

In the end his worry over the bill proved to be unfounded, the entire amount was covered by hospitalization. Unfortunately time would prove mine wasn't.

The day finally arrived when Jeff was released. He rode to the car in a wheelchair, then his father lifted him into the van. The doctor suggested putting him in the pool for his first attempt at standing, even he didn't know if this forced immobility might have done some permanent damage. "If he falls, the water will keep him from getting hurt."

Bill lowered him into the pool while we watched nervously. A few tentative steps, a short swim, and then slowly Jeff pulled himself up the wooden steps to dry ground. He could still walk.

Thankfully at the time it seemed as if nothing had been lost. I sent for a brochure on the bubble, determined to convince Bill it would be a worthwhile purchase. I couldn't forget how Jeff's legs had bothered him that past winter. We began a campaign to let Bill know how important we felt it would be, and finally he promised, "we'll get one when the overtime begins."

◆   ◆   ◆

When September came he not only ordered the bubble but bought a used gas heater to warm the pool water, and by Thanksgiving Day everything was in place. An impressive sight, a massive balloon-like dome covered the entire pool, at one end a blower kept it inflated, and a large slit that closed with a super-size zipper at the other end served as an entrance.

Now Jeff could swim everyday even though temperatures plummeted, but who had the time to swim with him? Bobby was working at the roller rink, and I knew Bill wouldn't even if he had the time. The logical solution was Petey, the youngest Klecan. He had spent much of the summer in the pool and was one of the few who spent time with Jeff. He readily agreed to come after school and from those hours spent with him a beautiful friendship grew. He became a brother, a friend, teacher and protector from then on, giving Jeff's life normalcy and meaning.

Bill, of course, resented Petey and didn't try to hide his true feelings, finding fault with everything he did. I felt it was a mixture of guilt and envy because he couldn't give Jeff the things Petey could. Although Petey seemed oblivious to Bill's innuendoes they galled me and more fuel was added to the resentment already burning inside.

As the holidays approached Bill announced, "Time to close down the pool."

"Why can't we keep it going till the New Year?"

"Don't be stupid! The heater might go out during the night, and the pipes freeze." he barked at me.

"They couldn't freeze that fast Besides it's worth the risk. Didn't you see how much worse Jeff felt when he wasn't swimming last year at this time?"

But my pleas fell on deaf ears. He was adamant. The bubble was deflated, the heater turned off. I couldn't understand why he wasn't willing to take any chance to keep Jeff going?

In spite of the closing of the pool Petey continued to come almost daily, they watched TV or played chess, Petey becoming like a member of the family.

Jeff's condition continued to deteriorate more rapidly during those next months, and I watched with dread as he fell more and more, deep down blaming Bill, at that time not admitting the accident may have been partially responsible.

When spring arrived and baseball season Jeff asked for the first time, "Could someone run for me? It makes me too tired."

I knew then a wheelchair would be needed in the not too distant future.

During his next checkup I said to the doctor, "I think the time has come to think about getting him a wheelchair. She took the necessary measurements and added, "He needs a youth' slim, so I'll have to order one." I saw no wheelchair that day, but when it was to be delivered I felt tense, unsure of what my reaction would be. The man who brought it called it the "Cadillac" of wheelchairs, bright, shiny chrome, upholstered in dark green simulated leather. A beauty and a horror, sitting. Waiting.

With the coming of spring the bubble went back up, but Jeff's laps in the pool were slower and fewer, and the bitterness towards Bill increased.

Another AOWs with Liz skating dance, figures, and freestyle. She was content competing; not caring if she ever won another championship. Bobby and Kathy were now skating dance, and though Bill went with us to Jersey he made it obvious he wasn't enjoying it.

The competition was held in April, but the winds of March still blew, proving too much for Jeff, a strong gust could topple him.

Back home he began sitting in the wheelchair now and then. It was easier. By the time school ended he was spending most his time in it at home, and I knew when he returned to school in the fall he'd no longer be walking.

22

A NEW CHALLENGE

Early that spring Pat, Bill's cousin's wife and I joined a "learn to bowl' league at the alley next to the roller rink, at the conclusion of which everyone who participated was presented with a pair of bowling shoes. When the children had no school we took them with us and let them bowl a few games, but the weight of the ball was too much for Jeff, knocking him over when he tried to throw it. It hurt so much to see him sitting, watching, when I knew how he wanted to bowl.

When he began using the wheelchair regularly I suggested he try bowling from that, and the sneer on his father's face told me what he thought of my idea. I ignored him and took Jeff to a small bowling alley in East Islip, Oscar's where I requested an end alley so as not to distract too many of the other bowlers, We were trying to figure out the best approach when a man who'd been standing behind us watching, stepped forward.

"Maybe I could help," he offered. "My name is Arnie." He helped direct Jeff in his chair to a position at the foul line and showed him how to hold the ball, then stepped back to where I stood.

I was to learn later he'd been a professional bowler until cancer in his leg forced him to retire, but his love for the game remained and he was determined to learn to bowl from the opposite side.

"How long has he been in the wheelchair?" he questioned.

"Approximately three weeks, not counting the times before he stopped walking." was my reply.

"It's amazing how well he manipulates it. You'd think he'd been using it for years," he added in astonishment. Then went on. "What he

97

needs is a light weight ball with five finger holes instead of the three so he can get a better grip. Let me find an alley ball that we can drill extra holes in and see if that helps."

The next time I took them to Oscar's the ball was ready. I knelt next to Jeff's chair at the foul line and held the ball in the palm of my hand till he had a firm grip. Then I'd slowly drop my hand, and he'd swing it back, forward, back again, then forward one more time letting it go. It rolled sluggishly down the alley and almost every time curved off into the gutter just before it reached the pins, or it stayed on the alley but came to a dead stop in front of the pins.

Watching, Arnie had another suggestion, "We could add a weight to keep it on the alley."

Jeff tried again with the weight and beamed when the first pin fell. He bowled a couple of games each week, gradually knocking down more and more pins, even getting a strike once in awhile. The pins would fall one at a time like a row of dominoes.

Dotty, Tony, Bill and I joined a summer bowling league. Our skating had died. Could this be any better? Even though we'd be part of a team, at least the actual bowling was individual, I reasoned with myself. Maybe it would work. We bowled one night a week, and I took the children another afternoon.

Between the time spent at the rink with Liz, home in the swimming pool, and bowling, the summer sped by. Labor Day arrived, and for the first time we tuned into the Jerry Lewis Telethon, which was inspiring and tear provoking. Jeff watched silently.

The few times we'd talked about what was happening to him I tried to make him feel good about himself. "I believe God made you this way because he knew you could handle it and would show others who aren't as strong how to make the most of what they have."

He never complained about the loss of ability to do things he'd once done, even stating, "I'm still not as bad off as someone who's blind."

How much he realized about the prognosis of the disease I didn't know. Was he aware his condition was usually fatal? He never mentioned what he saw that night on the telethon, and I felt I couldn't ask. But watching it made me want to do something to repay the Muscular Dystrophy Association for Jeff's wheelchair, and my announcement a few days later, "Let's have a carnival." was welcomed enthusiastically, and for the next three weeks our house was a beehive of activity. Petey, Jeff and Liz approached the local merchants with copies of a letter I'd written asking for donations for prizes, and they came home jubilant with their treasures.

A cake sale, make-shift games, a white elephant table and refreshments drew quite a few people. We darkened the garage to act out a spooky story, with props such as grapes for eyes, spaghetti for veins and scary background music, the birth of our spook houses.

We raised $340. which we mailed to Jerry Lewis. A fantastic sum we thought considering the short length of time spent on preparations. Plans for making the next one bigger and better were already forming in my mind.

School reopened a few days after the telethon and as expected Jeff could no longer walk, and he wasn't even twelve like the doctor had predicted.

A bus with a ramp was needed now, and when I requested he be returned to regular classes. the answer was, "His reading level is too low.

23

A VACATION

By spring Jeff could no longer stand for even a few minutes and each day became more dependent on me. Petey continued coming regularly and made sure he got out for more than just school. He took him in the wheelchair wherever they would have gone without it; to the end of Saxon into the Great South Bay, and on the frozen swamp behind our house, even falling through into a few inches of water where the ice was too thin.

That first Halloween Petey was pushing Jeff in the wheelchair trying to escape after they had egged someone, when they hit a patch of sand which stopped the chair abruptly, hurtling Jeff to the ground.

"Boy, that's the best time I've ever had on Halloween!" was his excited explosion when they arrived home.

For me that first year with the wheelchair was very difficult. Each morning I was awakened by a buzzer Bill had installed between our room and Jeff's, and sometimes I felt like screaming, "Leave me alone! I want to sleep a little more, I don't want to help you." But the words never left my mouth.

First I put on a pair of socks to keep his feet warm, next I pulled him to a sitting position on the edge of the bed, steadying him till he had his balance. From there I lifted him into his wheelchair, which he propelled into the bathroom where I switched him to the toilet. It distressed me to have to help him with the most personal things, wondering how he must feel and tried to ease any discomfort by gently teasing him.

I was physically and emotionally exhausted by the end of each day and fell into bed hoping Bill would go right to sleep. His sexual advances tolerated till then, in spite of the resentment boiling inside, were now dreaded. Many a night he fell asleep angry because though I tried, I couldn't hide my true feelings.

I looked forward to my hours spent with Liz at the rink. She was skating dance, mixed pairs, freestyle and figures, and even problems created by trying to get a nine-year-old girl to co-operate with a boy a few years older were welcome diversions.

"Why can't he learn to jump the same way I do?" she wanted to know, because she had been a left-handed jumper from the start. I was grateful for something to make me forget what awaited me at home.

At first I tried to get Bill to help with lifting Jeff but soon stopped when I saw how his displeasure upset Jeff.

After the New Year I began writing letters requesting donations for our next carnival which we were planning for the summer. With directories from Manhattan, Queens, Brooklyn and Nassau obtained from the phone company I made lists of manufacturers and distributors of everything from sunglasses to sport equipment. Next I mailed letters to all those on my lists. The responses were overwhelming—bicycles, bowling balls, cartons of toys, novelty hats, wallets, bottles of perfume and wine, to name a few. The United Parcel truck, or the "Ups" man as we called him, arrived every few days from spring into summer, turning our attic into a virtual warehouse.

◆   ◆   ◆

Liz qualified for Nationals in mixed pairs, dance and singles which meant a week in Jersey, a much needed respite for me. Since Bill wasn't taking any time off, Dotty had promised to help Bobby keep an eye on Jeff.

Just before we were to leave I received a phone call from Georgetown, Billy had been hospitalized with possible appendicitis and wanted me to fly to Washington. A conference by phone between Dr. Bernhardt and the physician attending Billy resulted in the advice, "Go with Liz to Jersey. Billy's a big boy now. His doctor says they couldn't find anything wrong. Probably just a case of nerves."

It happened just after the killings at Kent State and Billy had worked himself into a stew over the possibility of such a thing happening at Georgetown. He was released the next day.

◆   ◆   ◆

Once we were in South Amboy I realized how badly I needed a reprieve. It was 'heaven" to wake up in the morning and know Jeff wasn't waiting for me to get him out of bed. With each added duty, feelings of rebellion rose in me, but once I worked the new demands into my routine those feelings were forgotten.

A couple of nights after we arrived in Jersey a group of parents were sitting in the lounge discussing the events the day, and as they began drifting off to their rooms the father of one of the skaters asked, "Anyone care to have a nightcap with me in the bar?" Stupidly I agreed.

We talked about skating and our families over a couple of banana daiquiris, and it made me realize how badly I needed to talk to someone who actually listened.

Knowing the gossip mongers from the rink and not wanting to cause any problems the man stopped to see Bill on his return to Bayshore the next day, telling him about the drinks.

The following morning as Liz and I were about to order our breakfast in the dining room Bill came through the door pushing Jeff in the wheelchair. I felt utterly destroyed, my vacation was over. Bill knew once I saw Jeff it would be.

We had a terrible argument and for days after we returned home I felt depressed and edgy. On the way to the dentist's office with Liz one afternoon we were involved in an accident with the car in which Liz missed being seriously injured or killed by inches. It really shook me, I knew it had been my fault, my mind had not been on my driving.

It proved to be a turning point for me, I knew I had to do what I felt was right for Jeff, and learn to ignore what Bill did or said. It was obvious he was never going to accept things as they were.

24

PREPARATION

I busied myself with preparations for the carnival, typing individual letters for the children to deliver to the local merchants asking for donations. Never did I hear, "There's nothing to do." The youngsters in the neighborhood, along with Liz's cousins, Gina and Terry and their friend Susie congregated at our house, filled with ideas for a more productive carnival.

Jeff could have gone to a MD summer camp for a couple of weeks but preferred staying home, afraid he'd miss something, and I never encouraged him to spend time with the others with the same disease.

Petey, Liz and Jeff were a familiar sight that summer traipsing around Islip and Bayshore, letters in hand, canvassing merchants for donations, and returning jubilant over their riches; jewelry, toys, perfume and gift items. The anger over Bill's lack of support and the tears over Jeff's deterioration which I kept buried inside me most of the time, were dangerously close to the surface at carnival time, I was like a tinder box ready to ignite.

At the start of the summer even Bill caught the carnival fever. Always creative, he constructed games to be played for the many prizes donated; a penny pitch—a large flat board covered with squares slightly larger than a penny numbered from one to ten, another board set upright—circles drawn where inflated balloons were attached—targets for darts, a ring toss game—dowels glued upright on square blocks just large enough for the rings to fit over—the small prizes; pens, rings, sunglasses, even gift certificates secured to the dowels with rubber bands.

He built a wishing well big enough to hold a twenty-gallon trash container filled with water, and as I painted the plaque that was to hang from its roof, tears blinded me. It read, "He's Not Heavy, He's My Brother."

Dawn, Gina, Terri, Susie and Liz put together a water show selecting recordings of songs and making up routines to swim to. I sewed matching bathing suits for them, and Petey and Jack Corey helped with their comedy number. The two boys supposedly fishing, floated around in the pool in an inflatable boat with imitation fishing poles, a giant sandwich; a square foam pillow cut in half to resemble bread—slices of ham—cheese and lettuce—cut from appropriate colored fabrics. Liz, the fish, swam around the boat to the music "Baby, Don't Get Hooked On Me". One fisherman spotted her, poked the other, who poked back hard enough to capsize the boat. A wild chase followed, and when they finally caught their fish they put her up next to a measuring post then threw her back in, she was too small.

The show was a big hit and kept the participants busy for weeks rehearsing.

Another attraction was the spook house. Bill created a giant spider to hang from the ceiling, stapled tar paper over the windows to darken the garage, and made an assortment of scary creatures to hide in the corners. A sound effects record provided eerie noises in the background, and visitors were driven through a maze in a manual wheelchair. At one point the wheelchair was pushed onto what felt like railroad tracks and the sound of an approaching train filled the garage. The frightening screams heard from outside, and a few tearful guests spilling from its doors only increased the line of eager customers.

A couple of new faces were added to our crew. Teenage Sheila, pretty, long blonde hair, and even though badly afflicted with epilepsy, a talented acrobatic dancer. Watching her cope did much to encourage Jeff. My sister Peggy and her family, who had helped with our first carnival arrived ready to do whatever they could.

And there was Tom. A blond, good-looking young man about Pete's age. (The y had been dropped from Petey's name) Tom lived in the apartments built where the swamp had been. When he first arrived he was a little unsure of how to treat Jeff, but before long was playing basketball with him, using a soft sponge-like ball because a regulation one was too heavy for Jeff.

The tragic death of Tom's father had left him bitter, with what some called a real bad 'attitude', but watching him with Jeff I saw a sensitive, caring young man, and if Pete hadn't been Jeff's constant companion, I think it would have been Tom.

◆   ◆   ◆

The final touch for the carnival was a mammoth thermometer, red paint for the mercury that climbed as each new collection of money from the games and other attractions was counted and added to the total.

A ritual began that year, when the mercury reached the thousand dollar mark I was unceremoniously thrown, clothes and all into the pool.

Bobby laughed at us, too busy with his friends, Charlie, David, Joe and Sammy to be bothered with such nonsense.

The final total for the second carnival was almost $1500, which we again mailed to Jerry Lewis. Bobby was no longer laughing at us.

25

A NEAR TRAGEDY

A few days after the telethon school reopened. Bobby was now a senior, and I wondered if he'd make it to Graduation. He was still 'hanging out' with his group of friends, whom we'd labeled the "Mafia", who drank, played hooky and were constantly in some sort of petty trouble. Not bad enough to be considered juvenile delinquents but sufficient enough to give me many a sleepless night.

One night four of them piled into a car for a drive into the city. After parking, Bobby and David got separated from the others as they wandered around the streets, and when they returned to where the car had been, it was gone. With a policeman's help they found their way to Penn Station, from where Bobby called me about 6 a.m. to tell me they were waiting for a train to bring them home, their fares IOUs.

◆   ◆   ◆

We continued bowling, and for Jeff's birthday I bought a slightly used light-weight ball in the Pro Shop at Oscar's. The two extra holes were drilled in it, the weight added the same as it had been in the alley ball he'd been using, but when he tried rolling it down the alley it curved off into the gutter opposite from the one his old ball had.

"No problem, we'll just add a counter-weight," offered Arnie.

Several weeks later as Jeff's ball was coming back on the ball return, it hit the last uphill stretch and began rolling back down again. The same thing had happened with the old ball and we would just send another one after it to give it a push. But this time the balls connected with a resounding crack, and his new ball split in two. The whole process of drilling the extra holes had to be repeated with another ball. Couldn't anything be easy for him?

In spite of his bowling and guitar playing, by spring it was evident that MD hadn't let up, and Jeff's swimming slowed even more. Pete had taken him in the pool everyday until Bill closed it down near the end of November, but I kept silent this time.

◆   ◆   ◆

I started mailing letters for our next carnival early in January after learning some establishments had a limited amount of gifts and gave them out on a first come first serve basis. Donations once again flooded our house.

Bill joined a men's bowling league which met on Friday evenings, so we chose those nights to hold carnival meetings. He had made it obvious how much all the commotion annoyed him.

We still bowled together on Sunday nights in a mixed league with Dotty and Tony, but it hadn't proved any more enjoyable than skating because we still ended up fighting. If I got upset with myself when I bowled badly, Bill got angry.

One bright spot that spring was a visit to Westbury Music Fair to see Jerry Lewis perform, and after the show all the families with children in wheelchairs were invited backstage to meet Jerry. It was drafty, splashing rain and howling wind could be heard outside the exit door that stood slightly ajar. Almost half an hour passed before one of the many doors opened and Jerry emerged dressed in a monk-like robe. His words brought goose bumps to my arms. "Why didn't someone tell me "my kids" were waiting? Close that door," he snapped. "I don't want "my kids" catching cold."

He went to each family, exchanging a few words and shaking hands. I've never been thrilled by celebrities but was impressed with his obvious concern for the youngsters and his friendliness to all. Liz handed him a picture of the girls from the carnival water show.

"Do you have a copy?" he asked.

"No, but you can have this one, and we'll get another made," I assured him.

"No, you keep it and send me a copy when you get it."

He shook Jeff's hand, kissed Liz on the cheek and firmly squeezed my hand before moving on to the next family, and we returned home inspired to raise even more money to help his 'kids'.but our plans were interrupted almost tragically one morning late in May, when I was awakened at 6:10 a.m. by the sound of Jeff's buzzer. I stumbled sleepily from my bed and staggered into his room, muttering,

"What's wrong?"

"I don't know, something woke me, and I can't get back to sleep. Would you stay with me a while?" I sat on the edge of his bed brushing the hair from his face, "You probably just had a bad dream. Try and relax, and you'll fall asleep again."

Just then an ambulance sped past the house, siren wailing.

"There must have been an accident," I remarked as I mentally checked the whereabouts of everyone. The only one missing was Billy. Finished with his first year at Dowling, he hadn't wanted to return to Georgetown, he'd driven his used Ford Mustang to a friend's house in Oakdale, and they'd planned on fishing all night.

Suddenly the quiet was shattered by the jangling of the phone in the kitchen. Usually when it rang at such an early hour it meant someone needed a ride to work, or the lighting company wanted Bill to come in early, but as I raced to the kitchen I just knew it was bad news.

"This is the emergency room at Southside—"

The remainder of that morning was a blur until we arrived at the hospital and stood in the stark corridor outside Billy's room being questioned by the nurse, "Had he been drinking?"

All I could tell her was what his plans had been. I had no idea if they had been drinking. It had begun to rain, and he must have decided to head home. Later we learned he'd been about a mile from home when a car flew out of an intersection hitting him in the driver's side, totaling his car. He was lucky to be alive.

As I neared the hospital bed I was horrified, his face, swollen beyond recognition made him look like a creature from some scary movie, he was semi concious and groaning, and we were allowed to stay for only a couple of minutes.

The doctor was waiting, his words frightened me, "He's in pretty bad shape. I don't know if his right eye can be saved. The eye socket is like an eggshell, his is completely shattered and will have to be replaced with a plastic one. His jaw is broken and he's lost some teeth." The doctor put his arm around my shoulders and added, "It's in God's hands."

26

AN OPERATION

Each day the swelling receded a little until the doctor finally decided it was safe to operate. I worked numbly around the yard, unable to think about the possible outcome. Bill had gone to work.

Before the accident Liz had been preparing for States, to be held in Buffalo in early June, and each afternoon on my way to visit Billy I dropped her at the rink to practice. A few days before the operation she left with the Bonaguro family, she was scheduled to compete at the same time as Billy's operation.

Those hours seemed like an eternity, it was as if my brain had gone to sleep, and I remained like that until the doctor called to tell me Billy's eye would be all right

Later that evening Liz called, "I made finals but didn't place. I don't really care. I'm having so much fun." When they returned Mrs Bonaguro said, "She skated well, but something was missing. I think she really missed you."

I wondered if my being there would have made a difference. But I couldn't have gone knowing what Billy might have been facing.

After the operation, with all the swelling gone there was only a slight change in Billy's appearance, so insignificant only those who knew him real well were aware of it. There were minute scars, one at the edge of his eyebrow, and one just below the eye. He had to remain hospitalized for several weeks.

Donna, a girl he'd been seeing months prior to the accident paid regular visits to him while he was there, bearing cards and gifts, and the day he was released was at the house waiting.

"Billy, how do you feel about Donna?" I questioned after she left.

"Whatever was between us is over," was his reply.

"I'm afraid she has other ideas. All those visits to the hospital weren't just out of friendship. I think she'd like to patch things up."

He continued to be polite but cool to her, and I watched with a sinking heart as she turned her attention to Pete, constantly following him, including him in every project she was working on, and couldn't rid myself of the feeling she was using Pete as an excuse to spend more time at our house to be near Billy. Pete was just fifteen, Donna, eighteen and I watched as Pete's infatuation grew, helpless.

◆   ◆   ◆

The first item on our agenda at our initial carnival meeting after Billy's release was to set a date, and Donna begged, "I'm leaving for college on the fifteenth of August. Please have it before then?"

Usually we waited till the third week, but foolishly I complied with her wishes. We'd gotten started late because of the accident, and there was so much to be done. The youngsters hadn't even started their trips to the local merchants, posters had to be made, prizes sorted. I'd come to depend on Liz in spite of her young age. She organized each collection expedition, and every minute she wasn't at the rink she was working on some carnival project. But for everything she did, such as recording a song for the water show, Donna had some snide remark, "That music isn't right."

Pete etched a dragon on a tile for making tickets for the Chinese auctions, paint would be spread across the tile, slips of paper pressed on that, and when the paper was lifted just the image of the dragon would remain. Each paper had to be numbered, and then placed in an envelope with the numbers listed on the outside, and each envelop sold for a dollar. To make the covered boxes with slits in the tops in which these slips of paper would go look authentic Liz copied characters from a letter from a pen pal on them. Eight or ten boxes were placed on a long table with a prize along side; a clock, a bottle of wine, perfume, jewelry, a small appliance or a toy. After an hour or so a number would be drawn from each box, the prizes awarded by Jo and Nick who made their debuts as our official auctioneers. More prizes would replace them, and another auction would begin. Another addition that summer was a raffle for a pair of precision roller skates, a bicycle, and a bowling ball, all donations. A pony and a horse borrowed from Bill's cousin Kay, were kept with the Cummings permission, on their lot next to our house, for rides.

Bill painted life-size gay nineties figures on large boards, cut holes for faces, and one of the boys from the rink took pictures of people posing behind them.

Bobby, now a dedicated carnival worker along with his friends took over the spook house, but Billy showed no interest in anything, not unusual I was told after an accident such as his, "It will take awhile for him to get back to normal." Something his father couldn't understand and complained about constantly, "When's he going back to work? He's laid around long enough."

Bobby came up with the idea to borrow a casket for the spook house from his Uncle Roger, an undertaker. The day it was delivered Pete and I decided to play a trick on Bobby who was always doing something to me, such as leaving strange things in the refrigerator. Some examples, I'd find the entire Newsday stuffed in with the leftovers, a shoe or some other unlikely object nestled in with the lettuce.

The casket was a plain unadorned wooden box, shaped like a mummy's coffin, with a separate lid. Peter climbed in, lay down and I replaced the top, yelling, "Bobby, come quick! Uncle Roger sent us the wrong coffin. There's a body inside.!"

He bolted out the door, gingerly lifted the lid, and there lay Pete. An expression of horror appeared on his face momentarily, but was soon followed by hysterical laughter when he realized who it was.

For the spook house I made hooded gowns from material donated by Sol of the Farmers' Market, and Donna, adept with makeup, was to turn the spook house workers into gruesome creatures, and everyone begged to be one, especially the corpse in the coffin. In one corner an old horse's skull was placed with a red light glowing from within. Bobby was anxious to begin work on the garage weeks ahead of time, but his father barked, "You're not messing up my garage now, and I don't want tar paper stapled over the windows, you'll have to find another way to darken it."

No amount of pleading would get him to change his mind, even though he knew it was almost impossible to transform it into a convincing house of terror in just a few days.

27

CARNIVAL

At daybreak I awoke to the sound of the mockingbird's early morning serenade, but instead of one lone bird it sounded like the clear whistled chant of the tufted titmouse, the shrill of the blue jay and dozens of others greeting the day. Sitting on top of the telephone pole near the corner of the yard, he watched what looked like seven lumps just beginning to stir, sleeping bags arranged in a circle near the cherry tree, an empty wheelchair nearby. Carnival day had arrived.

The sleeping bags contained Liz, Pete, Gina, Terri, Jeff and two other carnival workers and every few seconds the mockingbird would lift straight up like a helicopter and land again, screaming and squawking at this intrusion.

I glanced around the gradually lightening yard, at the game booths sitting, wistfully waiting for the onslaught of excited crowds ready to try their luck, and colored banners flapping in the breeze expectantly.

I was standing near the window overlooking the driveway when I spied Bobby, face down, sound asleep on the hard cold concrete. We'd all worked through most of the night on the spook house, cardboard was taped over the windows, Bobby had even constructed a bridge with water under it, and one space was filled with pieces of foam rubber to give a strange sensation when you walked through it in the dark. When the rest of us had quit from exhaustion he'd said he had a few more things to finish.

Behind me the house was filled with prizes, all sorted and labeled, ready to be placed by each game.

I went outside, walked over to the sleeping bags from which issued sounds of giggling, and said, "Look what's over in the driveway."

They all scrambled up except Jeff, whom Pete helped me lift into his wheelchair.

"Ooh, my back hurts a little," he moaned. But had refused to miss the fun by sleeping in his comfortable bed.

"Come on, Bobby, its almost time to drive the water show stars around in the truck," I said nudging him with my foot.

The first to arrive to help were my sister Peggy, her husband Stan, and their children, Peggyanne, Junie, Denny and Beebee (Stan Jr.). Coming later with his band was Junie's boyfriend Tommy. Others began arriving, Donna with her overnight bag filled with makeup, my sister Jo with her family. I was helping Peggy and her crew set up the refreshment stand just outside the back door, corn-on-the-cob, soda, hamburgers, hot dogs, coffee and watermelon, all donations. Peggyanne was popping corn, Junie was putting it into boxes, and then the boxes into trays made from shallow cardboard boxes with ribbons attached to slip over the heads of the vendors. Dawn was husking corn, and Pete carrying out the prizes.

Questions flew from every direction, "Where's the butter?", "Do you know who has the tape?", "Are there any more balloons?"

Just then Liz stormed into the kitchen and burst into tears, a sign the carnival was taking its toll on her,

"Donna won't make me up. She says my eye might get infected." Liz had gotten up with one eye slightly swollen, and I'd told her to wash it with warm water.

I was beside myself already and almost screamed at her, "Go tell her I said to make you up as a witch!" She slammed out, only to return a few minutes later, crying, "She won't make me ugly. She says I have to be a pretty witch, I want to be scary like all the others."

I couldn't believe Donna, threw down what I had in my hand and marched out to where she was carefully applying makeup to one of the boys. "Donna, I want Liz made up as ugly as the rest of you. I'll be responsible for her eye. No arguments! There are more important things to be done than this silly bickering." I turned away not waiting for her reply and headed back to the house.

Bobby had come back out, climbed into the borrowed pickup truck covered with banners and balloons, and the girls jumped in for a ride around town to urge people to come to the carnival.

While they were gone final preparations were made. Already an hour before we were scheduled to open, a small crowd milled around in front of the tape stretched across the driveway. When the truck returned everyone went to their assigned spot, carpenter aprons on to hold money and tickets. The tape was removed, and the carnival began.

"Mom, Bobby took us down around Southside so Tony could see us," Liz informed me.

Tony had been hospitalized with a slight heart attack several days before, so Dotty wasn't going to be our clown as planned.

For the next two days there was a constant stream of people coming to see the performances of the water show, a long line that never seemed to shorten waited nervously to enter the spook house, the games were busy, and people crowded around to buy tickets for the Chinese auctions.

The money multiplied, and at the thousand dollar mark I found myself floundering in the pool, gratefully. The climax of the two days was an old fashioned auction presided over by Nick and Jo, where leftovers from everything were sold to the highest bidder. The wild bargaining of the crowd pushed the grand total even higher.

We had raised $2000., which we would send to Jerry Lewis. He had promised in a letter praising the work the youngsters were doing, which had arrived with an autographed picture a few days before, to mention our carnival on TV during the telethon.

An exhausted crew was faced with a tremendous cleanup job, games to be stored in the attic, the spook house to be dismantled, they yard raked, the pool and pool yard cleaned. The biggest job was mine getting the house back to normal.

A few days after the garage and yard was clean I invited Pete and Donna to a special going-away dinner for Donna, a dinner that turned into a disaster.

28

A CONFRONTATION

I wasn't too surprised when Donna announced as we presented her with a going-away gift, "I'm not leaving till the end of the month."

I felt she'd known this from the start but wanted us to have the carnival at her convenience.

"Let it slide," I thought, *"What good will it do to make an issue of it now? She'll be gone in a few weeks."*

We'd eaten in the garage, as we often did during the summer months, and Bill had gone bowling immediately afterwards. I was carrying in some dishes into the house when Katherine arrived, and Donna suggested a last walk around the neighborhood with Katherine and Pete. *"A little melodramatic,"* I thought. *It wasn't like it was her neighborhood, but that was typical."* Donna, Katherine and Pete started down the street, and Liz ran to catch up with them. I was on my way to the garage for another load of dishes when Liz raced back tears flowing down her face.

"Now what?" I asked impatiently.

"They don't want me," she cried.

I sat her down, listened to her tearful account and then waited for their return, and when they finally arrived I called to Donna from the house, "Donna, please come here, I want to talk to you." And as she entered, "Donna, I've put up with all I can take from you. You're so much older than Liz, and yet you deliberately tried to upset her all summer. She works very hard and I doubt that we'd be as successful without her. It wasn't very nice to make her feel unwanted," I scolded.

She turned on me, screaming, "She's a liar! We didn't tell her she couldn't walk with us!" Then slammed out the door and stalked down the street, Pete and Katherine in her wake.

It wasn't till a couple of days later that I began to suspect something was drastically wrong, there had been no word or sign from Pete, and Jeff was worried.

"Jeff, do you want me to call and see what's wrong?" I asked.

"Would you? I don't know why he doesn't come or call," he added, close to tears.

Pete wasn't home when I called, and his mother sounded cool and distant, "Pete's very upset over what happened at your home. Donna was extremely disturbed over your behavior. She said you started screaming at her as soon as she stepped through the door, Pete feels terrible."

Donna had convinced them she was the injured party. For my sake I didn't care, but Jeff would be lost without Pete. We did not hear from him till Donna left for school. I watched Jeff and wanted to cry, and when Pete did finally come there was a strain, he wasn't at ease with me as he had always been. Would things ever be the same again?

◆   ◆   ◆

Everyone who helped with the carnival was invited to spend the night of the telethon camped in front of our TV. They stretched out on the sofa, chairs and floor, some fell asleep quickly, others watched, dozed, awakened to watch again. Jeff's eyes were glued to the set whenever I glanced his way, and I wondered what was going through his mind.

◆   ◆   ◆

When school reopened a few days later Billy returned to his job but not to Dowling. Bobby was working in a gas station on the corner and taking police science at Suffolk Community College in Selden. Ironic, when I thought how often I'd worried he'd get into serious trouble himself.

He was 'going steady' with Debbie, whom he'd been seeing for some time, but he found holding down a job, attending classes and having a girlfriend too much and decided to drop out of school after the first semester.

Meanwhile a big change was to take place at the roller rink. Barbara and Carl announced at club on Sunday they were moving to North Carolina, where Carl would have his own rink. It was strange to think of life without the Hendersons.

There was a lot of talk among the skaters of leaving Bayshore, going to Levittown or taking up ice skating. Hearing that Liz pleaded with me to let her try ice. I knew she would hate being constantly pushed if we went to Levittown. Without telling her I did call an ice rink to see what such a move would involve.

A few days later during a dance lesson Barbara asked Liz about my call. The ice pro I'd spoken to knew the Hendersons and called them to inquire about Liz.

"Mom, please, can I ice skate? I always wanted to." she entreated.

"I called to see about lessons and found they're much more expensive, then there's the cost of ice time, and it'd mean a longer drive everyday. You know how you hate riding in the car. I haven't decided anything yet. Let's see what happens here first. You might like the new pro."

◆   ◆   ◆

Watching Liz practice one day I couldn't deny how fortunate I felt to have such a lovely daughter and much of it was due to Jeff's influence. As he grew older I knew how much I'd grown because of him. But what I hadn't realized was how many others outside our family had been affected by him.

Lisa, a girl Liz's age began skating at our rink and her mother introduced herself to me, "Barbara suggested I talk to you about Lisa's older sister. Barbara mentioned your son Jeff. Lisa's sister is sixteen now and has just learned she has Muscular Dystrophy. Do you mind if I ask some questions?"

We sat and talked while the two girls practiced and she told me how depressed Luanne was. Although her type of dystrophy wasn't fatal, Lauanne was finding it difficult to accept. Barbara seemed to feel if she met Jeff it might help. It sounded good, but I wondered how in one short visit she could see the acceptance and zest for life Jeff had shown the rest of us? But when I told Luanne's mother Jeff's reaction when I told him about Luanne, she was sure meeting him would make a difference.

"It's much harder for her, Jeff explained, "I was so little, and I've had more of a chance to get used to it."

He was extremely shy with strangers, and I knew he'd say very little to her when she came with her mother. We were working on props for the water show, and Jeff was struggling with the Chinese auction tickets. They stayed only about an hour, but that one short visit did light a spark, and many years later Luanne married and became the mother of a healthy baby boy. Or so we all thought at the time, then I met Luanne years later to learn she had three boys. Two out of the three had Duchenne MD the same as Jeff. She seemed to be coping very well and told me how she told her boys about Jeff all the time. I was saddened to learn about the two boys but at the same time impressed with her acceptance of her circumstances. I knew Jeff had been an inspiration to her.

◆   ◆   ◆

A young lady in her twenties arrived at the rink and began working with Carl, preparing to take over his freestyle students when he and Barbara left. She was newly married, pretty and a one-time world skater, and I watched as the other skaters and their parents went out of their way to impress her. I was wary, Liz had been with Carl for seven years, and the change wasn't going to be an easy one.

After Carl was gone I found my fears were unfounded, and we both fell in love with Kathy and her husband Rhett, who came to the rink with her quite often. Skating had been to Kathy; an escape, a refuge, an art and fun, and she saw much of herself in Liz. I was glad we'd stayed

◆　　　◆　　　◆

Meanwhile things at home weren't going well for Dotty and Tony. Several times that fall and winter our phone jarred me from a sound sleep late at night, "Could you drive Tony to the hospital? He doesn't feel at all well."

One night in April I drove him there for the last time, he died a couple of days later on the twenty-ninth, two days before his forty-sixth birthday, and after the funeral Dotty and her relatives all came to our house.

◆　　　◆　　　◆

Jeff's bowling was going so well he wanted to join a league. Pete, Dawn, Liz and Jeff joined together, and I, of course, went along to hand Jeff his ball. It didn't seem right to expect Liz or Pete to help him when they were bowling too, and I had tried unsuccessfully to get his father to accompany them. I didn't mind going, in fact, some of my happiest moments that summer were spent watching Jeff compete with normal youngsters.

One Saturday when they were bowling a man came up to me and asked, "How did you get him to bowl? I'd like to bring my son to watch, he sits home doing nothing all day. Would your son mind?" The telltale smirk on Jeff's face told me how pleased it made him and he commented "You told me I should set an example for others. You were right."

Their team ended up in last place, but it didn't matter because they really had a great time. Jeff was awarded a trophy for outstanding achievement, he'd impressed everyone with his determination and hard work.

But unfortunately we never did see the man again or his son. What a shame for a life to be wasted like that, I thought. How very sad. In spite of everything Jeff was enjoying life, and I know how much richer I was because of him.

29

MORE CHANGES

Billy displayed no interest in the carnival that summer, all he could think about was a proposed move to Florida in the fall to be near Sally, the girl he'd been dating.

The carnival was the largest we'd put together yet, and even Kathy and Rhett came to help. We expanded our idea of selling raffle tickets by going to the mall and large stores like Masters, where we met many nice people sympathetic to our cause.

Our garage was the center of activity where again tickets for the Chinese auctions were produced by whomever had free time and the inclination to work on them. There was always someone brushing paint on the tile, pressing slips of paper over it and spreading them around the table to dry. Jeff did his share even though it was painstakingly slow and tedious for him.

The water show had grown bigger and more complex, Liz's experience in skating shows proved a huge asset. She never stopped pushing the others. They practiced daily besides making the usual excursions for donations.

We also held a bowl-a-thon at Oscar's, which helped push our total over the $2000. mark that year. Because of the large amount we'd sent the year before we were asked to appear on the telethon to present our check, imagine our disappointment when we learned Jerry Lewis wouldn't be on the New York portion of the show; he would be in Las Vegas.

We were told to be in the studio in the city by ten a.m. on Labor Day. Bobby offered to drive us, so of course, we were late getting started, and it was a wild and bumpy ride. When we spotted the build-ing there was no place to park so Bobby pulled up to the sidewalk, unloaded Jeff and I then went to find a place to leave the van while we went on in.

Liz and Pete were sent to sit in the audience in a small cramped stu-dio where Bobby joined them. I'd planned on Liz and Pete doing the talking but found Jeff and myself face to face with the M.C. I managed to explain how we'd raised the money, handed him the check, and breathed a sigh of relief when we were on our way back home.

We did see Jerry that fall at the Westbury Music Fair, and backstage after the show I handed Jerry the enlarged, autographed picture of the girls from the water show.

"It took you long enough," he exclaimed grinning in his own inimi-table way.

Back at the rink preparations were under way for another show. Kathy, an artist and a skater made a sketch of the dress she wanted me to make for Liz, sky blue, white ruffles at the wrists and peeking from beneath the bottom of the skirt, and her music, "On a Clear Day You Can See Forever." Four of the teenage boys accompanied her to make it a small production number.

It was to be Kathy's only show and Liz's last at Bayshore.

Kathy had come to teach figures and freestyle, but the couple who were to teach dance didn't want to share the spotlight and made her so uncomfortable she resigned at the end of her first year.

That year with Kathy had been one of the happiest for Liz. Kathy sensed Liz's love for skating, and a beautiful relationship flowered between them, and Kathy and Rhett helped bring back some of Liz's joy in skating. Over the years since she'd won "Tiny Tots" much of the fun had been lost because she was the ONE to beat, and each new skater felt they had to be better than she was, even though she hadn't won a championship since.

◆   ◆   ◆

Kathy's leaving was a terrible blow to us. What should we do now? We didn't want to stay, and I doubted Liz would be happy in Levittown where she'd be pushed constantly. She could give up skating entirely or give ice a try. There wasn't much doubt as to what her choice would be. So we bade farewell to the world of roller skating and prepared for our first trip to the Royal Ice Rink in Kings Park on the northern side of Long Island.

30

A WELCOME TWIST

Neither of us were too sure how we were going to like the change. Her first day on ice she could hardly contain her excitement, wanted to try everything she'd ever done on roller skates. "It's easier to get round on my jumps but harder to land them without falling. I go so fast when I spin, it makes me dizzy," she laughed.

The pro who was to give her lessons warned her about her speed, "Give yourself a chance to get used to it." But her intoxication overcame her caution, and when we headed home after the session she had a large lump on her right knee.

Neither the ride, which almost discouraged her at first, nor the throbbing bump could dampen her enthusiasm. As time passed and some of the novelty wore off the drive was no longer a problem, confirming the feeling I'd had that extreme excitement combined with the movement of the car was the real cause of the car sickness.

Her new pro, Leslie didn't believe in competition, and the idea of Liz skating just for fun suited me fine. Our lives had taken a welcome twist. I'd enjoyed the past year at the roller rink, except for Kathy's unhappiness. She kept in touch, even going to watch Liz ice skate and remarked, "She's a natural on ice."

It was also a relief not to have to watch what I said at home. It bothered me that Jeff was alone so much, though he didn't seem to mind. He had guitar to practice, home-work to do, could still use the phone and was able to get in and out of the house if he wanted to. Pete was in his last year of high school and though things were closer to normal, didn't have much time to spend with Jeff.

At one point the school psychologist requested a meeting with Jeff's dad. Knowing Bill would refuse if I asked him to go, I faced him with, "On your way home from work tomorrow you're supposed to stop at school to see the psychologist."

"What's she want?" he asked gruffly.

She didn't say, just that it's important."

Hope fluttered like a butterfly, maybe she'd get through to him. I waited patiently for him to get home that day and when he did, "It was a waste, she's an idiot," were his only comments.

At my next visit I inquired, "What did Jeff's father say?"

From the little I could get from him I'd say don't expect his support. He can't face what's happening to his son."

◆   ◆   ◆

A strange phenomena occurred when we began going to the ice rink, Bill became more and more involved at the roller rink, the place he claimed he hated, and when they needed help to apply the plastic to the skating surface or if there was any carpentry work to be done, he was there.

◆   ◆   ◆

The Royal Ice Rink was a purely recreational rink, yet the undercurrents of competition were there. Karen, a girl about Liz's age had been taking lessons from another pro, and the two of them were disturbed by Liz's appearance on the scene. Until then Karen had commanded the attention of the spectators because she had been the only skater advanced enough to spin and do a few simple jumps. Karen's pro began trying to teach Karen everything she saw Leslie teaching Liz, which only made Liz laugh. This was nothing compared to what she'd already experienced in roller skating.

When a nearby competitive rink was unavailable for those who practiced and took lessons there, they flocked to Royal. Watching them, I was glad we were no longer involved in that way.

◆   ◆   ◆

At Christmas time the ground was covered with snow, temperatures dropped well below freezing, perfect for the ice rink behind the house. On what had been our patio before the swimming pool was installed I laid a large sheet of heavy plastic, approximately ten by twenty feet, put six inch high aluminum edging around the outside and with the plastic pulled up over the top clamped it in place with spring-type clothes pins, and then flooded it with water, each night adding more as it froze. As soon as Liz got home from the rink she was whirling around on it.

Kathy and Rhett came for a Christmas visit, and immediately following dinner Kathy and Liz were on the ice like two school children.

◆   ◆   ◆

At the rink Liz began taking ISIA (Ice Skating Institute of America) tests. She passed each of the three preliminary tests with no difficulty. Meanwhile Leslie and the other pro were putting together a show, and I volunteered to help with the costumes. After the elaborate shows at the roller rink this was very different, there were no large rehearsals, no props, and the costumes consisted of leotards with the addition of a skirt or sleeves to make it more show-like, most with only a sequin design which I added.

Liz and Karen, now friends, performed one number together and each had a solo. Liz had chosen The Entertainer for her music and was a striking picture in a red sequined outfit, with her long blond hair flowing round her as she glided across the ice.

Lessons continued with Leslie, and for a Christmas exhibition Liz, in an outfit of white chiffon and sequins, skated to It's a Marshmallow World. Following the holidays Liz was again disappointed, Leslie decided to resign, and Liz shed indignant tears.

31

HOOKED AGAIN

"What am I going to do now?" wailed Liz. "I'm not taking lessons from MaryLou."

"I should hope not. Why don't you just skate on your own for awhile? See what happens, don't make any decisions yet," I suggested.

Several weeks went by, and Liz became friendly with Jeannie Carr, a pro from the Long Island Arena, who had been coming to Royal with some of her students.

"Mom, can I take from Jeannie" she finally asked.

"It's up to you. Give it a try if you want, and if it doesn't work out you can always find another pro."

I liked Jeannie but had some reservations, she believed in competition, and before long she convinced Liz to give it a try.

We'd had a year's rest from that kind of life, and I wasn't overjoyed at the prospect of starting again. There were advantages though, skating became more exciting, a challenge. Jeannie wanted to prepare Liz for the Nassau County Championships in March, which meant Liz had to take her preliminary figure test to qualify. (This was a different test than those she'd taken in Kings Park.)

She found figures on ice more stimulating than they'd been in roller skating. Roller skating figures were done on painted circles on the floor, but on ice the skater had to make her own tracings with the strokes of her blades, then follow this thin line for the remainder of the figure, and every deviation was glaringly obvious. There were instances where judges actually got on their knees to study the tracings. In order to practice figures a patch of ice had to be rented, and with one lesson on how to do the required figures and a week of patch-time, Liz was ready.

We made the trip to Roll N' Ice, a dreary, cold place, on a snowy wintry morning. You entered the rink by climbing a flight of stairs, going through a door, then another and down more steps into a large room, bare except for a rickety table and three wooden benches chewed by countless skated blades. The floor was covered with black rubber interlocking tiles. *Feel like you're in a subway,* I thought.

On one wall was a window that opened into a small room, more like a closet, a large mirror along the back wall and shelves beneath cluttered with lost mittens, sweaters, papers and books. A coffee maker sat on the sill of the opening. Hanging on hooks on the wall to the left was an assortment of skating outfits. The door opened upward and was fastened to a hook in the ceiling.

On another wall in the large room was a long window which opened the same way :the Pro Shop, holding all the paraphernalia needed for skating. Figure and hockey. Boots, blades, tape for the hockey players, laces and a machine for sharpening skates. Opposite was a door leading to the ladies' room, a dirty dingy place everyone avoided, if possible. The skating surface itself was beyond a garage-type door, with windows through which spectators could watch. A regular size door led to the ice. With enough floor space to hold a bench, a record player and a shed-like structure where the Zamboni was kept. The floor between the entrance and the ice felt as it was about to cave in any minute.

The ice surface was small, bumpy, with overhead pipes that dropped particles of rust onto it. There was a feeling of cold, dampness and dirt.

Most of this escaped us on that first venture there because we were too excited over Liz's first test on ice before real judges. The ISIA tests had been judged by the pros at Royal.

The other girls were nervous and fidgety, but Liz waited calmly till it was her turn to go on the ice, and I stood on one of the benches set against the wall alongside the ice, shivering from the cold and anticipation, watching

One of the other girl's pros came to stand beside me, "She's really having a good time, isn't she?" More of a statement than a question.

"Yes, she is." Thinking *I wonder if it'll last?* She'd begun figures on roller skates with the same enthusiasm but had come to dislike them.

That day she passed with exceptionally high marks, in spite of the short length of time she'd worked on the figures, and we left the rink looking forward with great anticipation to her first ice competition to be held in Cantiaque Park in Hicksville several weeks later.

Cantiaque was a county-owned park with swimming pools, baseball field, a golf course and a golf driving range, clean and well kept. As it had been in roller skating, competitors arrived, hair combed and curled, with their fancy outfits, polished skates and the air was filled with tension.

It was a pleasure to see that slim figure flying around the ice to the music Jeannie had picked for her program, and the first place trophy only added to it. Bill came, after Liz begged and couldn't hide his delight at the results. We were hooked again! Jeannie was already planning for the next competition in July.

Taking lessons from Jeannie meant going to the Commack Arena a couple of days a week besides the three at Royal. It was expensive, but I tried to keep it under control. Thousands of dollars could easily be spent in a few months on this sport and were by many. We couldn't hope to compete with girls whose fathers were doctors, businessmen and lawyers.

Liz missed out on many school activities but never complained, and I felt proud to see how well liked she was. Even those with preconceived notions that she was spoiled because of the attention soon changed their minds when they got to know her.

◆   ◆   ◆

One Sunday afternoon we'd gone for a ride in the van and stopped at a hot dog stand, a wave of nausea washed over me when I saw Jeff sitting in the back unsuccessfully attempting to lift his soda to his lips.Fighting panic, I tried to explain it away, "Your arms are tired from playing ball." I couldn't let him know how frightened I really was.

But as the days passed it was evident his arms were much weaker, but thankfully it didn't affect his bowling then.

He'd gone from a slightly plump little boy to a too thin teenager; the wasting muscles no longer giving the impression of health, and I was stunned when Bill accused me of not feeding him properly.

Jeff practiced his guitar less and less, until one day he looked at me sadly and said, "Mom, I don't feel like taking lessons anymore. It's too tiring."

The frustration and sadness I felt made me determined to make even more money with a bigger and better carnival that summer. I knew time was running out.

32

MATT

So much was going on that spring and summer I didn't have time to dwell on my growing fear for Jeff. Billy and Sally had returned to Bayshore and were finalizing their wedding plans for the twenty-fifth of May, with Liz a junior bridesmaid, and Jeff the ring bearer. Sally had picked out the bridesmaids' dresses but even the smallest was too large for Liz.

"I can get you the material if you would care to make her dress yourself," the salesgirl apprised me. I knew with a little improvisation on a pattern I found a few days later I could make the dress look exactly like the others.

"Mom, Sally would rather you had the dress from the store altered," Billy informed me when I showed him.

"But why? It's not a difficult dress to make. Did you tell her how much sewing I've done?"

"I tried, but she still would feel better if you got the other one."

Rather than create a problem I paid an additional sixty dollars, plus the cost of the dress on a gown I could have made for half the price of the alterations alone

The ceremony took place at St. Mark's Episcopal Church in Islip where Bobby and Billy had sung in the junior choir, and I'd taught Sunday School. Billy and Sally left for the airport for their flight back to Florida following a reception at Flynn's Restaurant.

◆   ◆   ◆

A new family moved into the neighborhood that summer, the Crawfords, Howard and Pat, their three daughters, Patti, Judy and Nancy, and their son Howie. Their house was built next door on what had been part of Cummings' property until they retired, sold their house and moved to the farm in Salem.

Howard and Bill became good friends, constantly calling to each other across the fence,

"Look at the size of this tomato," Howard's voice would boom.

"That's a midget compared to mine. Feast your eyes on this baby!" Bill would throw back at him, waving an even larger one high in the air. This went on with each variety they grew.

The following spring after Bill put in his tomato plants Howard sneaked over and tied red Christmas balls on each one.

There was a loud "What the hell's going on?" when Bill discovered them.

Liz became the Crawford's official baby sitter, and as the children grew she'd come home commenting, "They don't need a sitter, they need a referee."

◆   ◆   ◆

June brought Pete's graduation and a job working in the traffic sign department for the town, which left little time to spend with Jeff and even less for the carnival.

Kathy Gallow, a friend from the roller rink taught Liz a variety of moves that could be incorporated into their swimming routines—backward and forward rolls and surface dives with the swimmers holding their legs in a diverse number of positions. She also brought some new recruits, her sister, Loretta, brother Tommy and another roller skater Bobby Lee. With him came his friend Matt, along with several others. Now there were twelve in the water show.

Matt had many of the same traits as Pete, specifically, his desire to make Jeff feel like everyone else. He helped in every phase of the carnival, staying days on end, without ever going home to sleep.

Our acceptance of Jeff and his problems had grown over the years, and I'd forgotten how frightening it'd been in the beginning. None of us realized how much we'd changed, and people meeting us for the first time marveled that we treated Jeff as if were a normal teenager. But Matt, like Pete saw him just that way from the start.

For our newest carnival attraction we held a beauty contest, applications were printed, and about a dozen little girls registered. I made a purple velvet cape, trimmed with white fake fur and covered a cardboard crown with aluminum foil and artificial rubies, diamonds, sapphires, and pearls.

Although I wasn't consciously thinking about Jeff's decline it was always there just below the surface. At carnival time my emotions were in a turmoil. One day just prior to the big day Liz was trying to polish one of the water show numbers, a couple of the boys would not stop horsing around, and when I came out by the pool and saw her getting upset I began to tremble. "We're doing this to raise money to save lives not just to have a good time. What we raise could mean a chance for Jeff to live longer than the few year's he's supposed to." Tears slipped down my cheeks with this outburst, and then feeling remorseful for being so harsh I retreated into the house.

A few minutes later I heard Liz come through the back door and call, "Mom, where are you?"

"I'm in my room." I was sitting at my desk, my face in my hands.

"Matt had a big fight with those guys over what you said. He felt really bad that they had upset you so."

"Oh great! Now I feel even worse. I shouldn't expect others to feel the way we do about the carnivals. Everything's been building inside, and it made me furious to see them giving you a hard time."

"Don't feel bad. Maybe it was a good thing you blew up. If you hadn't, I probably would have."

The weekend dragged by with no word from Matt, and when he did come he carried a bird house he'd built for me, and it took him a few hours before he was his usual animated self again.

But I couldn't shake the feeling of culpability, and hoping to rectify my oppressive actions wrote a note to Matt's mom, and a few days later received this letter.

Dear Mrs Eldredge,

Thank you for your kind words in the midst of your own deep suffering. I have seen the pain in your eyes and I really did not know how to respond to it. Friendship is a mutual relationship and Jeff is a gift in Matt's life. We are all meant to be gifts to one another, the world is beautiful even though there is so much pain and suffering—so much of the beauty that we see comes through the love and concern we share with others.

When I read your letter I was overwhelmed with emotion and have not cried so much since I was nine years old and my father died. Every situation and relationship is bittersweet and so tears are often a mixture of joy and sorrow. Sorrow for the intensity of your pain and joy that Matt would have touched the life of another in a way that s real meaning. I pray only that each one of my children (there are eight) will be loving and compassionate and open to the infinite possibilities of each and every person they meet. I want them to see with the eyes of the heart that they know what real life is all about.

How could Jeff help but be a happy boy, you have gone beyond your own suffering and chosen to live life fully for him and with him. Not every child is graced with that kind of love from parents.

I had hoped that you would not feel we were indifferent to Matt since we allowed him to stay away from home so often, if you have felt any holding back on my part that was my only concern.

I allowed Matt to read your letter and savor all of it. A few times I tried to discuss Jeff's illness with Matt, I was very gentle because I didn't know how openly the problem is discussed. Your letter has given me the freedom to be totally open with Matt so that his whole future relationship with Jeff will be especially rich and full.

So many parents faced with tragedy are overcome with self-pity allowing each precious moment to slip by. I admire your courage.

For each of us the precious gift of life is over in what seems a blinking of an eye, no one of us can be sure of more than the present moment and length of life doesn't determine the quality of life. The meaning of life is to be found in the choices we make. We can celebrate the light or curse the darkness.

I am happy that Matt and Jeff are friends and that Matt gives you joy too.

The way we live gives an added dimension of meaning to life. How different our world would be if we were not afraid to be as open about the way life finishes as we are about so many other things. I am being open with you because it is the way I feel

Matt was in a lot of pain Saturday. We all were, he found it hard to handle his frustration until he busied himself building a bird house and going door to door to try to sell the patches (interfacing I cut in shapes of dogs, ice cream cones, skates and many other objects, covered them completely with sequins, for putting on sweaters and jeans.) *Jeff will live on in Matt's heart forever and ever.*

Matt is not morbid nor am I, we try to be real.

Thank you for allowing us to share the intimacy of grief in your life. How can we ever repay you for all that your example gives to us. In the book "Brothers Kamarzon" there is a line that says, "you shall embrace the earth and water it with your tears of joy."—joy is suffering overcome.

May your tears be tears of joy in the sure knowledge that you have lived life to its fullest

Peace and courage too,

Winnie Clark.

33

POWER

With Matt's mother's letter came the boost I needed, we raised more money than with any other carnival, and never seen Jeff work harder. A check well over $2000. was presented at a dance marathon held at the Smith Haven Mall on Labor Day, part of the telethon.

I almost hated to see that summer end, but there was to be a bright spot for Jeff in school, his class moved to the Islip Junior High, and he was put in with the slower "normal" students with two men teachers.

On the not so positive side Jeff, Liz, Mat and Matt's sister Laura joined the Saturday morning bowling league, and I watched Jeff's bowling gradually deteriorate. Though his average never very high sank lower each week, he never complained. I also noticed he was having more difficulty maneuvering his wheelchair.

"I think it's time we looked into the possibility of getting Jeff a motorized chair," I mentioned to Bill one night as we were getting into bed.

"Who's going to pay for that?" he wanted to know.

"Maybe we could use some of the money he got from his accident," I suggested.

"You're always so worried about spoiling him. Aren't you afraid you're encouraging him to be lazy?"

Upset by his attitude I replied, "No. He tires much quicker than he used to. Why should he use what little energy he has for just getting around? Just think of all the freedom he'd have with a chair he could operate entirely on his own."

"Humph, you're the expert as usual." he added curtly as he turned over to go to sleep.

◆　　　◆　　　◆

"Jeff, what would you think of using some of your savings for buying a wheelchair with a motor?" I asked the next day.

"How much will it cost?"

"I'm going to call MD and find out. Maybe they'll even help pay for it."

"If it doesn't cost too much," he worried as he turned his attention back to the ballgame he was watching.

◆　　　◆　　　◆

"We'll give you what a manual chair would cost, and you'll have to make up the difference," the lady at MD advised me when I called.

But there was an obstacle. "I'm sorry, that money can't be touched until Jeff is twenty-one," explained my lawyer.

"But that's crazy! He probably won't even live till then," and went on to explain Jeff's situation. "Isn't there some way he could be allowed to use the money to make his life more pleasant now?" I pleaded.

"I didn't realize his condition was that serious. I'll see what can be done. We'll probably have to go through the courts," he added apologetically.

Bill had constructed a folding ramp to get Jeff and his chair into the van, but I knew the new chair would be much heavier, and doubted I could get it up the ramp with Jeff in it. I found where hydraulic lifts for vans were manufactured and decided since MDA was paying for part of the chair we'd put the money we didn't have to use for that towards a lift.

As soon as the lawyer called to tell me the judge had ruled in our favor we ordered both, and a youth-size, extra narrow wheelchair arrived late in November, about a week later the lift, which Bill and Nick installed in the rear of the van.

The chair, upholstered in dark green, had a left-handed control with a switch long enough so Jeff could manipulate the chair backwards, forward and in either direction with pressure from his fingers. Two car-sized batteries in a metal case were suspended between the large rear wheels, wires running to small cylindrical motors on each side just below the arm rest.

Within a few days Jeff had mastered the chair, by no means an insignificant achievement, but wanted no part of the protruding footrests. "They slow me down too much," he complained.

We all made an attempt to operate his new chair but found it almost impossible to keep under control.

Jeff's condition wasn't the only thing deteriorating, the relationship between Bill and I seemed hopeless. His biggest complaint was, "Why can't we be a normal family?" especially when we were working on the carnival, or I was driving one or the other to some kind of lesson.

I began to dread coming home, was glad when he worked late, and when he was home I kept busy with carnival work, making skating dresses, painting; anything to keep occupied.

He was perpetually angry with me, everything I did was an annoyance and only when an outsider was present was he civil to me. When he wasn't grumbling he was silent, which was almost worse. I'd be waiting for the explosion that I knew was coming.

Whenever there was a social event, a family wedding or party I'd find him lying on the bed complaining of a headache, and if we did go I felt lonely and envious of those enjoying themselves. I'd think, just the other day Mrs. Klecan told me she envied me because Bill did so much around the house, always building or redoing something, but how I wished he'd do less and take time to enjoy his home and family.

One night as we were preparing to bowl at the alley a man from one of the other teams came up to where we were standing, and said, "I want you to know you've done a wonderful job with your son. I've been watching him on Saturdays mornings, and he's something to see."

Bill, voice filled with malice, jerked his head in my direction and replied, "It wasn't me, *she* did it!" then stalked away, leaving me standing there feeling mortified.

But the man ignoring his rudeness went on, "I've been watching that series on Willowbrook on the news. Does your son live at home?"

I tried to answer his questions and hide my hurt and confusion, thinking how different things could have been. Why couldn't Jeff's problems have brought us closer? I wondered.

34

QUESTIONS

As spring tulips and daffodils gave way to roses, carnival preparations bloomed in our lives. Matt came almost daily, helping with the carnival or just having fun with Jeff, he'd hop into one of the non-motorized wheelchairs, and they'd play soccer in the driveway.

This angered Bill, "He's going to wreck that chair," he'd shoot at me and then turn and yell, "That's not a toy."

I shook my head in disbelief wondering how he could put the value of a chair over the obvious pleasure Jeff was getting from having Matt on his level? When Bill wasn't around I encouraged it.

One afternoon Matt, Liz and Jeff were going to Masters for some poster-board, and they all used wheelchairs instead of walking. Jeff in his motorized one, Matt and Liz in manual chairs, and when they returned they were almost hysterical.

"We went single file, like a train. When we got to the store Jeff went first, then I hooked my feet under the back of his chair, and Matt did the same behind me. Jeff towed us up and down the aisles," Liz described their adventure laughing.

"You should have seen everyone staring. It was great!" Jeff added wickedly.

"The best part was when we went to the stationary store, Liz got up from her wheelchair to open the door for us. This old broad standing there almost fell on her face," was Matt's contribution.

On another occasion Liz, her cousin Terri and Jeff set out to buy paint for posters they were working on. The two girls filled their pockets with crab apples from our front yard, then walked slowly, chatting, while Jeff sped on ahead. Then the girls started tossing the apples at Jeff's wheels, and a man passing in his car gaped at this spectacle, drove down the block, turned around, came back and stopped next to the girls. "What do you think you're doing to that poor soul? he scolded. "How could you pick on someone like that? he demanded angrily, at which the girls burst into fits of giggling.

"It's all right. He's not a poor soul, he's my brother, "Liz assured the flabbergasted man.

"Having Jeff sure makes life more fun," was Liz's comment when she related the incident on their arrival home. "But I felt kind of sorry for that poor man, he was pretty upset." added Terri.

◆　　　◆　　　◆

Bill seemed to have lost all interest in the carnival. He spent his free time in his garden, workshop or bowling. On Friday night after Liz and Jeff had gone to bed, and Bill was at the bowling alley I sat at the long table in the garage working on posters when a car pulled in the driveway, and Bobby hurried in.

"There's something screwy going on. Debbie's supposed to be baby sitting, but when I call the house there's no answer."

"If you're really worried why don't you take a ride over there?"

"I guess I will," he threw back as he headed back to his car, and left for Debbie's house.

A few minutes later Bill arrived, "You spending the night out here?" he chided.

"I just want to finish these posters for tomorrow. We're selling chances at Burger King. We should do really well. How'd you bowl?"

"Fine," he snorted as he slammed into the house.

Another half hour passed, the headlights of Bobby's car swung into the driveway, and he burst into the garage. Cold fingers of fear gripped me as he erupted into tears.

"Did something happen to Debbie?"

He shook his head, words stumbling out jerkily, "Debbie's fine, I just misunderstood where she was baby sitting. It's Jeff. It's so unfair. He's never done anything bad or mean, he loves everyone and asks for so little. Why is this happening to him?"

"Think about it. Jeff's happy. How many really happy people do you know? He's accepted what's happening, and you should too. Jeff has always gotten joy from the simplest things. Who else do you know who gets excited over a present of new underwear?"

A smile flickered across Bobby's face at my last remark.

"He doesn't have to have anything else. What brought this on?" I asked.

"It's selling those chances at Fairchilds. Everyone's asking me about Jeff and Muscular Dystrophy. I don't usually give it much thought, but it's been hard this past week."

"I could question too, but never have. Take one day at a time and try not to think too far ahead. It's not always easy. Think about all the fun we've had with the carnivals, and the great people we've met because of your brother."

He came around to where I was sitting and put his arms around me, "Thanks, Mom, I feel a little better." He sat beside me and we talked long into the night, remembering the good times and bad. It was well after three when I crawled into bed, a grumble greeted me, "Doesn't anyone believe in sleep around here?"

◆   ◆   ◆

Our day at Burger King proved successful in several ways, we sold hundreds of chances, and with the girls dressed in their water show outfits, taking turns wearing the beauty queen cape and crown we signed up many contestants for our beauty pageant.

But for Jeff it was an even bigger day, he decided to make his first solo trip for any distance in his new chair. Burger King was about three-quarters of a mile from home, and he had to cross a main thoroughfare, the railroad tracks and another busy intersection. I had qualms but couldn't let him know.

When enough time for him to have reached home had elapsed, it seemed an eternity, Liz called to find him very pleased with himself. But of course, his father was furious with me for allowing it.

◆   ◆   ◆

It wasn't till a day or two before the carnival that Bill decided to join in our efforts. Always looking for new ways to include Jeff, I suggested having him pull some sort of a ride with his wheelchair around the front yard where we would set up a zoo of neighborhood animals; birds, turtles, dogs and cats.

Bill worried about the strain on Jeff's motors, but when we agreed he'd pull only the smallest youngsters he designed and built a small cart, and I found an engineer's cap, red with big white circles for Jeff to wear.

That along with our usual attractions helped make another carnival another huge success, over $2000. was raised again. During the two days of the carnival Bill strutted around as if he'd masterminded the entire thing, but I didn't care.

35

THE SUFFOLK ROYALS

There was another change in schools for Jeff that fall, but not a welcome one, he was moved to a different junior high, about a twenty minute ride from home. The remainder of the special class was moving to Terryville, an even longer drive, for vocational training, but because of the weakness in Jeff's arms they felt it wasn't practical for him.

"Why can't he continue here in this junior high? He was so happy this past year," I questioned the psychologist.

Again I was given some vague excuse for not letting him stay. "He's going to BOCES (Board of Cooperative Education) in Sayville, where he'll pursue an academic program." And earn, I thought, a high school diploma.

◆　　　◆　　　◆

Things weren't getting any better at home. I tried to avoid antagonizing Bill, without success. Our trips to the rink were relaxing, I'd read, knit or just watch Liz skate. We dreaded going home, and would often remain chatting with the rink employees after Liz was finished. Especially Ricky, one of the skate guards, and his sister Kathy who worked behind the snack bar. Ricky was a big tease, he'd skate around calling me Mom, and had people believing he was Liz's brother.

As we said our good-byes one afternoon I thought I detected a sly look on his face, and when we arrived at the van we found an assortment of rubbish stuffed under the windshield wipers; an old paper plate, a candy wrapper, leaves and a discarded work of art done by some small child.

It explained Ricky's expression, so I carefully removed each item, put them in the van and drove home. The next time we went to the rink I asked the manager to page Ricky to the office.

"Ricky, report to the office," boomed a voice over the loudspeaker down by the ice.

"What's this?" he asked with a puzzled look when I handed him a brightly wrapped box as he entered. "Open it,"

He ripped off the paper, lifted the lid and stood gaping at his gift wrapped litter.

◆   ◆   ◆

Sometimes we stayed to watch a hockey team made up of boys between the ages of fifteen and twenty practice. They competed in the Met League and played every Sunday evening at Royal Ice Rink, now called Superior. One afternoon Liz suggested, "Why don't we bring Jeff to one of their games?"

"Might be fun, and it'd get him out with more people."

But when I asked him he was hesitant. "I don't know, I don't really watch hockey that much."

"We'll go to one game, and if you don't like it we won't go again."

"Hockey! Can't you people ever stay home?" was Bill's reaction.

"You could go with us," I advised.

"I've got too much to do."

◆   ◆   ◆

When we arrived at the rink we went through the lobby, then a pair of doors to a long ramp that led to the ice. Jeff steered his way down and parked next to the glass at the blue line, and in the beginning I stood next to him while Liz climbed up on the bleachers behind. The first game wasn't too clear to me, but Jeff watched intensely. Mr. Ahrens and his wife, parents of Boomer (Glen), one of the defense men, explained "off sides", "icing" and penalties to Jeff, and whenever Boomer was sent to the penalty box by the referee his mother would plead to no-one in particular, "He didn't mean to do it."

After the game the owner of the rink came to us, and asked Jeff, "Would you like to meet the players?" He handed him a blue spiral book, adding, "You can keep track of the stats with this score book, and we hope you'll come to all our games."

Jeff beamed when the players came up after their showers and autographed the first page of his book as they were introduced to him, some were hesitant.

On our arrival home Jeff was overflowing with excitement, "Look Dad, they gave me a score book, all the players signed it, and they asked me to come to all their games."

Bill just shook his head in disgust.

◆   ◆   ◆

Our weekly trips to the Royal's games began, a blossoming romance with the game of hockey and a ritual of waiting to talk to the players after the game.

His favorite, though he liked them all, was Mike Labianca, a fast, sure skater with a high scoring ability. Mike gave Jeff his phone number so he could call to see how the team fared when they played in Jersey, Brooklyn or Westchester.

Lynn, sister of one of the players, who announced the penalties and goals asked him to keep track of shots on goal and supplied him with the lineups of both teams before the games.

We saw only part of that first season, but it opened up a whole new world to Jeff, and he could hardly wait for the new season to start.

◆   ◆   ◆

Summer flew by with another carnival, Bills moods increasingly erratic.

One night after supper Liz, Jeff, Bobby and I were embroiled in an animated game of Monopoly when suddenly in a rage, supposedly over someone taking a bite out of his first green pepper from his garden, but more likely because we were having fun, Bill grabbed the Monopoly board, scattering the pieces in every corner of the room. Jeff's poodle, Mr. Chet, always ready to protect Jeff, sprang up only to be kicked with such force he sailed into the wall whimpering.

Somehow I got the trembling Jeff, along with Bobby and Liz into the garage where we sat huddled together for almost an hour before I tentatively sneaked into the house only to find Bill in bed, fast asleep. The next day he made no mention of what had happened.

As we prepared for the carnival that summer Bill not only offered no assistance but complained constantly about having it. "Why can't you people act normal? Why do you have to get involved in this every year?"

I had to admit it was a lot of hard work and made a wreck of the house, but I felt it was so good for Jeff, making him feel he was doing his share. Our newest addition that year was a trampoline borrowed from a boys' club by Sheila, the girl from Liz's dance school. She supervised its use, showing each person who purchased a ticket a few of the basic moves, and even I spent hours on it during the carnival and for the two weeks it remained in the yard afterwards

Our biggest contributor of prizes that year was the Garcia company; a pair of skis, fishing poles and rods, six aluminum tennis rackets, and all kinds of camping equipment.

During the two days of the carnival Bill again paraded around giving the impression he'd been all for it from the start and a few days later returned home from work to announce he'd been made a United

Fund representative because of all the money *he'd* raised with the carnivals.

36

ENVY DIES

Christine, the second oldest daughter of Bill's cousin Danny, was married at the end of the summer. She had suffered with convulsions beginning in high school, had been diagnosed as epileptic, and it taken her years to adjust. Now she was a glowing bride. At times I felt a twinge of envy thinking, *"At least there is a medication to control it."*

◆   ◆   ◆

Another school year arrived and again Jeff was moved, to a BOCES class in Shoreham, an hour and a half ride each way. He complained, but only about being tired from the long ride, seemed relatively happy, and the reports from his teachers were encouraging. There were times when he got extremely upset over the actions of the other students, especially the day one poked something into his tire, causing a flat. But he had the Royals which made everything else less important.

Liz also made a move, she'd gradually become disenchanted with Jeannie and wanted to take lessons from someone else.

"Get out of here, this rink isn't competitive enough for you," Liz was advised.

Beebee Riggs who taught at Roll 'N Ice was recommended. So I phoned the dreary hole of a rink where Liz had taken her preliminary test. As it turned out, in spite of its appearance there were a few good things about skating there—the lower cost of ice, the regular patch time everyday and the more regimented atmosphere. Her figures became the most important thing to her, and she quickly passed her first and second tests. She also joined a precision skating team, the Racquettes, a group of sixteen girls who skated a program in unison. This meant a trip to Racquet and Rink in Farmingdale once a week for practice. We were now making daily trips to Copaigue, a weekly trip to Superior and an added one to Farmingdale.

◆   ◆   ◆

A couple of months after Christine's wedding she had a seizure different than any she'd had before, for a brief time she couldn't speak or move one arm, and tests uncovered a brain tumor. A few days after her twenty-sixth birthday the doctors removed as much of the malignant growth as they could, and months of hospitalization followed.

One cold afternoon I dropped Liz at the rink and went with Chris' mother, Pat, on the train to visit Chris in University Hospital in New York City. The combination of the tests and the operation had left her paralyzed on one side and unable to speak. She had just begun to say a few words again, haltingly, but her happy smile told me she was glad I'd come.

In the past I'd often called Pat when I needed someone to talk to, but now when I phoned her it was to lend support. Chris would remain in the hospital for months of chemotherapy and rehabilitation.

◆   ◆   ◆

We attended every Royal home game that season, Bobby often going with us, and I watched Jeff try to break out of his prison of shyness. For his fifteenth birthday I bought him a Royal jacket. He'd become a fixture by the boards, players and fans expecting to see him there. When he got involved in the game he momentarily forgot his timidity, and just as a semi-hush would settle over the rink he'd shout, "You're a fucking asshole!" at the referee.

Sitting in the stands with Liz now, I'd pull up the collar of my coat and mutter, "I don't know him."

The other fans loved it when he got so agitated, "That's it Jeff. Let 'em have it!"

◆   ◆   ◆

In May Chris was released from the hospital and went home to her apartment in Queens with her husband, but a few days later he called her mother and asked if he could bring Chris back to her, he couldn't handle her.

I stopped in to see them whenever I could, Chris' face lit up whenever she saw me. She couldn't walk, spoke hesitantly and clung to my hand when I was there. A return trip to the hospital for tests showed the tumor had grown back rapidly, and Chris was given only a few months to live. My envy had long since vanished.

◆   ◆   ◆

By the end of the season the Royals were contenders for the championship, their last regular season game was to be played in Jersey. Bobby agreed to drive us, and as soon as he finished work at Fairchilds in Farmingdale he picked us up. Jeff was still quite slim and Bobby lifted him easily into his car and folded the manual chair, putting it in the trunk.

It was a "nail biter" of a game with the Royals and Westsiders battling all the way. The Royals were out front in the third period till the Westsiders tied the score when a penalty was called. Because of the point totals a tie was the same as a loss to the Royals.

The final buzzer sounded, no goal, no championship.

I quickly made my way to where Jeff sat at the far end of the rink. My eyes reached him first; he sat head bowed, but when he looked up and saw me he let the clip board and cow bell he held fall to the floor, and I could see traces of tears on his face. The teams he rooted for always seemed to lose, but I wasn't going to let him give into the despair I knew he was feeling.

As I reached where he sat I said, "Jeff, I know how rotten you feel but think of the players."

Dropping his head again he murmured, "I'm sorry, I was being selfish. Would you push me to where the players come off the ice?"

They came one by one after the Westsiders were presented with the trophy, tears glistening on some faces, others cursing softly.

"Don't feel bad, you guys played well. That last call by the ref was a really bad one, they never should have had that power play," Jeff managed to force out, still fighting his own disappointment.

◆   ◆   ◆

Now the season was over it was time to concentrate once more on getting things ready for the carnival. I'd been working on mermaid tails for the water show, so I worked on them at the rink while Liz practiced, sewing sequins in a scalloped pattern on aqua spandex to resemble scales. The first attempt to swim in one of the tails, funny as it was at the time could have been disastrous. Liz dove into the deep end of the pool, and the tail filled with water, making it almost impossible to surface. Luckily she was a strong swimmer and made it to the shallow end where I cut holes in the bottom to allow water to escape.

Then I had to find a way to keep the fins from collapsing into a pile of wet polyester, and after unsuccessfully using hanger wire, Pete home on a visit from Brooklyn, where he'd moved the year before to be near his job in the veterans' hospital, solved the problem with pieces of heavy flexible plastic, a quarter of an inch thick, that I cut in the shape of fins and then inserted.

Swimming in the tails was difficult and took long hours of practice. The opening number began with a mermaid in each corner of the pool, and they swam to the Beatles' music *The Otopuses Garden* from their album Yellow Submarine.

◆ ◆ ◆

While talking to Pete he remarked, "I wish we could go back to the days when Jeff and I were together all the time, they were the best."

Girls and dating had taken Matt from us though he came to see Jeff once in awhile. I kept Jeff busy making tickets for the Chinese auctions.

◆ ◆ ◆

Bobby and Debbie, engaged now, had set a date for their wedding, found an apartment and put a down payment on furniture, then three weeks before the big day Bobby announced, "Debbie needs more time, she isn't sure she's ready for marriage.' A couple of weeks went by and Bobby decided she was right and they called it off.

◆ ◆ ◆

When the carnival and summer were over Jeff returned to school at Shoreham, and just before their first Royal game of the new season he asked, "Could we go watch the Royals practice on Friday nights?"

The players were very happy to see him, and one of them skated over to Jeff's spot by the boards and reached over the glass to shake his hand, a look of disbelief shot across Larry's face when he realized Jeff could not even lift his hand up to his. I knew Jeff was as distressed as Larry, because he knew he'd upset him.

After the first game one of the players suggested, "Why don't you come on the bus with us to our next away game?"

So began our wild Fridays when Liz and I would race home from practice, have Bill's dinner on the table, and then Liz, Jeff and I would fly across the island to catch the team bus. Between Norm, the coach, and Mr Pavese, the father of two of the players they carried Jeff onto the bus and sat him in a front seat next to me. I would stretch one arm across in front of him because he was afraid he'd lose his balance if the bus made an abrupt stop. His wheelchair was folded and stowed in with the hockey equipment underneath.

Stupidly, I still tried to include Bill, offering an account of each trip, hoping he'd see how much the games meant to Jeff.

◆   ◆   ◆

Bill was spending more and more time at the roller rink, doing carpentry work or any other odd job that needed to be done, sometimes starting as late as eleven-thirty at night.

Bobby starting his new landscaping business advertised in the <u>Pennysaver,</u> and one morning I took a call from one of his customers, Mrs. Barton. During our conversation she asked, "Do you know of anyone who'd like to earn a few dollars sitting with my collie?"

After further questioning I offered to do it myself. She was an elderly woman who lived alone except for her dog, in a secluded house surrounded by a high chain link fence, the gate kept padlocked at all times. I spent a few hours a week with her friendly, affectionate dog while she ran errands.

But when I came home filled with stories of servants and huge parties she described from the old days and told of the deepest, largest in-ground pool I'd ever seen, but now empty, Bill got annoyed. "Why do you have to go there? Don't you have enough to keep you busy?"

I had filled my time with enough to keep me from mourning an empty marriage, and although everything I did was for or with the children, Bill accused me of looking for someone to replace him.

Then one night he came home from the rink and told me, "Pete is looking for someone to work a few nights a week in the cashier's booth. He asked if you would be interested."

The cost of ice had risen, the pro's fees were going up steadily, and I knew I'd make more than what I did for Mrs. Barton, but she was upset when I told her I wouldn't be coming anymore.

I hated to leave her but felt working at the rink might ease some of the tension at home. Since Bill was spending so much of his time there, at least he wouldn't have to worry about what I was doing.

I missed being home with Liz and Jeff but told myself it was only a couple of nights, and I could still take Jeff to games.

◆   ◆   ◆

The Royals were having a fantastic year, and it looked like they were headed for the championship, but fate stepped in, and we were to miss all but one game of the playoffs.

37

FEAR AND HOPE

It was Friday, and because Bill didn't like the van sitting in the parking lot while I worked, afraid some of the rowdier skaters who spent their weekends there might do some damage to it, he dropped me at the rink and took the van home with him. When the session ended I counted the cash, typed my financial statement for Pete, and Bill arrived to take me home. During the drive silence prevailed, and after I hopped from the van he went back to the rink to do some work.

Earlier in the day I'd driven Liz and a girlfriend Shari who was to spend the weekend home from practice. Now the three of us sat talking while I waited for Jeff to announce he was ready for me to put him into bed. As usual, he was watching sports on TV. After I'd gotten him settled I said goodnight to everyone and crawled into bed.

◆   ◆   ◆

A loud knocking woke me. Glancing sleepily at the clock I saw I'd only been asleep about an hour. I stumbled out of bed pulling on my robe and called through the back door, "Who is it?"

"It's me, Jimmy. There's been an accident," came back the voice of the rink custodian.

I yanked open the door, my heart pounding wildly.

"Bill fell, hit his head and his leg is burned. He's out in the van. I just wanted to tell you I was taking him to Southside."

"I'll come as soon as I can," I said tensely, my mind racing in circles. *No sense in scaring the girls and Jeff, call Dotty, got to find Bobby, Where'd he say they were going?* I grabbed the phone, dialing Dotty's number. She would be right over. *Now think! What's the name of that bar where they hang out? Sand something.* Nervously I picked at the cuticle on my finger, *Sand—Piper, that's it.* I seized the phone book, *what to look under?* I turned to the Yellow Pages, B-Bar, Bar Supplies, *no restaurant.*

I found the number and dialed. It rang, three, four times before I heard music and a voice at the other end.

"Is Bobby Eldredge there?"

"Let me check," a wait that seemed interminable, "Sorry, he just left to take someone home. Said he'd be right back."

"Please tell him to call home immediately. This is his mother. It's an emergency!" I prayed as I hung up that this wouldn't be one of those times Bobby got lost for hours. I threw on the clothes I'd taken off only a couple of hours before, shivering.

Within minutes Dotty was at the door. "Bobby just pulled in the driveway," she told me as she came into the kitchen.

Bobby burst in, "What's wrong? Is it Jeff? The bartender said you called."

"No, its your father. He fell at the rink, hitting his head, and Jimmy said the torch he was using to remove the old tiles set fire to his pants. Thank God Jimmy was still there! Dotty, we'll be back as soon as we can," I added, turning to her as she took off her coat.

"Don't worry. You know me, I don't sleep anyway."

Bobby and I dashed out to his car and within minutes were at Southside just outside the emergency room. The nurse led us to where Bill lay moaning, in a great deal of pain but aware of our presence. One look at his leg and faintness edged at my consciousness, and the nurse took my arm, guiding me back to the waiting room. Bobby remained for a few more minutes, then came toward me pale and shaken.

"His blood pressure just shot way up. After they treat his leg they're taking him to a room. The doctor says there is no sense in our staying any longer. He said to call in the morning," Bobby informed me when he joined me.

At the nurse's request we went to the admittance office before going into the cold night air and driving home in silence.

Back at the house Bobby got out a bottle, poured amber liquid into a glass, handing it to me and said, "Here, Mom, drink this, it'll help you sleep."

As the liquor burned my throat I sputtered, but it did enable me to fall asleep almost immediately. I woke early, wondering what to tell Liz and Jeff. I heard giggling coming from the girls' room. *Stay calm, don't scare them too much,* I cautioned myself, as I tapped on the door. "Liz, could I talk to you for a minute?"

"Sure, come on in," her voice danced behind the door.

But when she saw me the dance stopped, "Mom, whats wrong? You don't look good. Are you sick?"

"There was an accident last night. Your father's in Southside. He—"

"Is he going to be all right? How much damage to the van?" she almost screamed at me.

"He wasn't in the van. He fell at the rink and burned his leg with the torch he was using. But I'm sure he'll be OK." I tried to reassure her. "I'm going to call the hospital now and see how he is."

"Can I go see him?" she pleaded.

"I'll find out when I call what the visiting hours are."

She stood by me as I dialed the number, fidgeting nervously.

The voice coming at me from the phone didn't make sense. "He's in intensive care. He had a bad night."

Oh God, what's happening? I didn't think the burn was that bad. A strong feeling of foreboding crept in, and I tried to sound calm as I explained we could only see him for a few minutes.

"We'll go as soon as I get Jeff up and dressed."

Jeff wanted to wait at home. "I'll go next time."

So Bobby, Liz and I rushed down to the hospital. "Immediate Family Only" read the sign on the door, and I glanced fearfully at Bobby.

We entered a large sterile room sectioned off with curtains, life sustaining machines clicking and whirring all around us, and what looked like TV monitors by most of the beds, and in a bed in one corner Bill lay quietly, metal rails pulled up at the sides. He smiled slightly, but when he talked he seemed confused, didn't seem to know why he was there. *What was wrong?*

His forehead and nose were badly scraped, *He must have hit his face on the cement wall by the men's room when he fell,* I thought.

We stayed our allotted few minutes and then drove back home, and as we pulled in the driveway I broke the silence, "I'll call Dr. Bernhardt, he'll know what's wrong."

Several hours later when I finally got to talk to him he informed me, "He's acting very strangely. I've called in a specialist. There's more than just the burn on his leg. He seems confused."

On our next visit we were greeted by a neurosurgeon, "I'm afraid he's had a cerebral hemorrhage. A blood vessel going to his brain has erupted. Tests will be done when we're sure his condition's stable. The hemorrhage must have caused the fall."

It was then I recalled Bobby's words about his father's blood pressure shooting up in the emergency room. Maybe the hemorrhage had occurred then. Possibly the fumes from the heat of the torch and melting glue had caused the fall. Not that it really mattered now. But Jimmy had said Bill had directed him to the emergency room, and he seemed clearheaded but in pain when we saw him there.

"Usually a person has this condition from birth, and doesn't survive past thirty. We'll do tests to see if surgery is possible. I'm warning you now, this is very serious. He's an extremely sick man, and there is the definite possibility he might not make it."

We listened in shocked silence. *This isn't real. He's telling us he might die.*

Our visit with Bill immediately following only emphasized his words. Bill didn't remember that we'd been there earlier. "I'm staying till it gets warm out," he announced.

How unlike him.

Our few minutes were soon up, and as we left the hospital a few snow flakes fluttered down. Again I called Dr. Bernhardt. "Have you called Billy?" he inquired.

"I just told him his father was in the hospital and left it up to him whether or not he made the trip. Billy and Sally are buying a house, and I didn't know if he could afford to fly home. I didn't know how serious it was then." "Call him back and tell him if he wants to see his father again he'd better get here." Another call to Florida and a promise he'd be on the first flight he could get.

♦   ♦   ♦

The next week was spent running to the hospital only to find Bill more confused and disoriented. I tried to keep our lives operating smoothly. I'd send Liz and Jeff to school, make the beds, straighten or vacuum, run to the hospital and be home when they returned to take Liz to practice. Then after supper we'd all visit him again.

Billy arrived, alone. Sally not only didn't want to come but tried to persuade him not to, "Your father's not **that** sick."

Thursday arrived, St. Patrick's Day, my birthday, but there was no celebration. Liz and I went to the gift shop where she picked out a leprechaun doll for her father, and they named him Luigi, Bill's mother was of Italian extract.

Saturday Bill was moved from ICU to a semi-private room. *Encouraging. He might still make it.* We went to visit him and found him in better spirits than he'd been in a long time.

The tests were scheduled for Tuesday morning.

When I described some of Bill's violent outbursts to the neurosurgeon, he explained, "Pressure could have built up causing such behavior. Any emotional upheaval could have triggered them. It's very possible he didn't even remember his actions afterwards."

It could explain so much. Maybe this was the turning point, if his condition was behind his behavior it could also be the basis for so many things wrong in our lives. *Let the operation change all that*, I prayed. *Things could be so different.*

Before we left for home Bill asked us to bring the Sunday paper, TV Guide and Carvel when we came the next day. My spirits soared.

38

THREES

On Sunday, a bright sunny day, we all piled in the van for the ride to Southside, filled with hope. At first everything seemed fine, Bill asked about the temperature outside and what'd been happening at home, then suddenly, "The rabbits and carrots are going round and round," spurted from his mouth.

What was he saying? We sat stupefied.

Liz broke the spell, taking the ice cream from the bag, scooping some onto the spoon, she handed it to him but he couldn't hold on to it and dropped it before he could get it to his mouth. Liz quickly picked up the spoon and proceeded to feed it to him. A glance at Jeff's stricken face, and I led him into the hall where tears streamed down his face.

Bobby followed, "Mom, what's wrong? Why is he talking crazy? He seemed so much better."

"I don't know. Let me see if I can find the doctor."

At the nurses' station I asked if the doctor was in the hospital. "I'll see if I can get him for you," offered one of the nurses.

While we waited Billy placed a call to Florida, and it was evident from his stilted replies there was some disagreement.

"Mom, I'm flying back tonight.

The doctor arrived and explained, "There's still some bleeding. We're going to do an angeogram on Tuesday to find out what we're faced with."

As we walked to the car Liz burst into tears, and I put my arm around her shaking shoulders, at loss for words.

Billy flew back to Florida that night, and I held back a plea to stay until at least after the tests were completed because I hadn't forgotten the stroke Chis had suffered during those same tests. Would they be too much for Bill?

My visit to the hospital the next afternoon alone only added to my growing fear. He was quiet, sleeping most of the time.

"Wake him and try to get him to eat." pleaded the nurse.

I fed him silently, waking him each time he dozed off.

I left there completely dejected, the doctor's last words ringing in my ears, "No Visitors! You and only you are to see him. I don't like what's happening."

That night Bobby went with me, "I'll wait in the hall. Call me if you need me."

Bill didn't seem to know I was even there, and the next afternoon they told me he wasn't back from the tests and to come back at supper time. Bobby accompanied me again.

"A couple of weeks' rest, and we'll operated," was the doctor's answer to my questions about the results of the tests.

On Wednesday I went back hoping for some improvement, but he lay staring into space, slipping in and out of consciousness, and I held his hand praying, "Please come through this," and for a brief second I thought I felt slight pressure from his hand in response.

On Thursday there was no sign of communication or recognition, I could feel him slipping away. Friday he slept as if in a cataleptic state.

◆   ◆   ◆

When Bobby came home from work he urged me to take Liz and Jeff to the opening game of the playoffs at Superior.

"I can't, I have to try to get your father to eat."

"Mom, I'll go feed him. You need a break."

Reluctantly I agreed, but every time an announcement came over the loudspeaker at the rink I froze. didn't know who they played, who won, and we didn't stay to see the players.

When we got home Bobby was waiting, "He's not going to make it!" he cried.

"Why, did something happen?" Terror gripped me.

"No, the nurse told me. She wanted to talk to you this afternoon but said you looked so upset when you were leaving she didn't have the heart to tell you. They found another aneurysm on the other side, ready to burst like the first one. One of them is out of reach surgically. There's nothing they can do."

We held each other, our tears mingling.

◆　　　◆　　　◆

Saturday morning the ringing of the phone tore me from bed, and as I picked up the receiver and heard the words I knew. He was gone.

◆　　　◆　　　◆

The next few days were a blur.

Billy arrived back, alone.

The funeral home filled with flowers; from the roller rink clubs of Bayshore and Levittown, the many people from the ice rinks, the Suffolk Royals, another from the players' parents, the people we'd met bowling, our neighbors, Bill's co-workers, bosses and relatives. The room was crowded with people, a stream of faces speaking of the gentle, caring man they'd known, blame rippled just below the surface, resentment or was I imagining it? Bill's brother had been angry when the doctor refused to let anyone visit during that last week.

They hadn't known the side of him, sometimes violent, other times cruel, how he had wounded those closest to him. Didn't know of the times I'd thought of leaving, but remembering my own fatherless childhood stayed, thinking "Any father is better than none at all." The dreams I'd had of when Jeff finally lost his battle of my walking away, that I woke from with tears on my face. I was truly sorry things had ended like this.

I shed no tears, except at home, till I looked at his face for the last time before the casket was closed for the trip to the church. Twenty-seven years. Some good memories but so much heartache and loneliness were buried with him that spring-like day. He'd kept his promise, he stayed till it got warm.

◆   ◆   ◆

When we arrived home Jeff started up the ramp to the front door, but half-way his chair began to pull to one side, refusing to go straight, and for the first time since the night Bobby had told us Bill was dying, tears gushed from Jeff's eyes. "Why doesn't this damn chair work right? he railed through the flood.

I released the back levers that held the belts tight to make it easier to push the chair manually. "I'll call Pasco. They will fix it."

Bobby lifted Jeff into his other chair while I called Patchogue Surgical, and they promised to send someone right away. Liz and I set the table with the food we'd prepared for those coming back to the house, and waited. My sisters arrived, more time passed. Elsie, Bills stepmother came for a few minutes but didn't stay. I understood, Bill's father had been buried on the same date exactly four years earlier.

My sisters, their families Jeff, Bobby, Billy and I ate, wondering where everyone else was. Pat and Danny had Chris to worry about, she still clung to life, but where were all the others? Then the phone rang, and a voice chased everything else from my mind.

"I'm going to Pat and Danny's. Christine just died."

◆   ◆   ◆

A repetition of the week before. The same room, in the same funeral home, many of the same faces, another ride in the hated black limousine, an open grave next to one piled high with wilting flowers, and Chris, Bill's goddaughter was buried beside him.

◆   ◆   ◆

My mother always swore things happened in threes. A few days later my sister Peg called, her husband Stan had suffered a stroke that had paralyzed one side of his body and left him without speech, and I prayed that was the third and final catastrophe.

39

A PARTY

There was so much to be done. Since Bill hadn't left a will the two older boys agreed to sign everything over to me. The insurance money seemed like an enormous amount, and yet I knew with only Social Security coming in it would melt quickly if I weren't careful. Even though Bill had been with LILCO for almost twenty-five years there was no pension. He had to be at least fifty-five when he died and would have been forty-seven that April.

About a week after Chris' funeral, her mother called to ask if I wanted to ride with her to the Social Security office. She had to straighten out Chris' affairs, and I hadn't filed for survivor's benefits yet.

I t was during the ride to Patchogue I learned why I'd been snubbed on the day of Bill's funeral, someone had circulated a story that I had been cheating on Bill. I cannot honestly say I wasn't tempted, but loneliness could be endured, the welfare of my children came first.

◆   ◆   ◆

I was determined we'd show everyone we could survive without any help but was to find in the days ahead a few of Bill's family did care about us. His Uncle Karl called often, offering advise on how to handle what little money I had, showing his understanding of the strain a disabled child could put on a marriage. He had a son with Cerebral Palsy. And Bill's sister Marlene and her family included us in their Thanksgiving that fall, and of course, I knew Pat and Danny were there if we needed them.

Even though it made me nervous spending what seemed such a large sum of money, I ordered a new black van with a fiberglass top, at Bobby's and Liz's urging.

In the months ahead I found it difficult to fall asleep at night, would toss and turn till I finally dozed off, then wake in the morning my mind racing from problem to problem, always coming back to money. But I wasn't the only one frightened, Jeff watched me like a hawk, worried if I complained of fatigue or some ache or pain. It'd take a long time before he lost the apprehension that something was going to happen to me.

As concerned as I was about finances I felt Liz's skating was even more important now. Her father's death had hit her hard. She'd gotten extremely upset when his belongings were returned from the hospital, and Luigi was missing. Tears came easily now.

Most of the skaters at Roll n Ice were getting ready to leave for summer skating camp with Beebee. I considered sending Liz too, but the expense and the thought of her away for the entire summer soon chased the idea from my mind.

Liz had gone to Roll n Ice expecting to begin lessons with Beebee, but her mother insisted her daughter was too busy, and Liz was to take from her instead. Liz resented being made to wait and didn't like the idea of taking from the mother who hadn't even skated herself, feeling she wasn't qualified to teach. Lessons with Beebee finally began just before Beebee's departure for camp. Rather than return to Mrs Riggs I took Liz to Twin Rinks in Port Washington once a week for lessons with another pro. She still did her practicing at Roll n Ice. The move to the other pro did not ingratiate her with Mrs Riggs who made things almost unbearable, such as giving Liz the worst patch of ice for figure practice, so when the summer ended we moved to Racquet n Rink in Farmingdale. Port Washington was too far to travel every day and much too expensive.

At home we cleaned up the unfinished projects Bill had left and tried to get the yard in shape. When September arrived Jeff was sent to yet another school, that I hoped was going to be better because it was only a twenty-minute ride from home. But Jeff began complaining he wasn't learning anything and was being threatened physically by one of the other students.

I had been a member of the <u>Committee on the Handicapped</u> in Islip schools for a few years, and along with Jo, another member, felt we weren't contributing anything worthwhile to it. At the end of the previous year we'd decided when school reopened in the fall we'd familiarize ourselves with the various facilities where the handicapped students from our district were being sent, and Jeff's complaints made us elect to begin with his class.

We had some trouble finding our way into the school, and when we asked a school bus driver for directions she remarked, "Oh, you're looking for the retards."

Inside the school we couldn't locate the room where the class was supposed to be and on questioning a few of the students in the hallway we were told, "We don't know of any such class."

We had been assured that these young people, including Jeff were being mainstreamed; mixing in with the regular students, yet these "normal" pupils didn't even know they existed. In the office we were finally told they were in prefabs tacked on to the rear of the school.

Although we went as committee members the teachers knew I was Jeff's mother. One teacher began her explanation of the class and its occupants. "The kids in this class can't learn anymore than they already know, they do not know where they belong when the bell rings,—and though they claim they can read none can."

"Are you talking about Jeff?"

"Oh no, he's an exception," was the quick reply.

"Then what's he doing here?"

No answer.

After a few more remarks by the teachers we made our way to the exit. Jo turned to me as we walked to the car, "I don't believe it. What's he doing there? Did you see the size of those guys and hear their language? They scared me, and I'm not helpless like Jeff."

I was too upset to reply.

As soon as I was home the tears flowed, as did the questions. "*What had I done to him? Why hadn't I fought to get him back with normal students?* That I didn't expect him to live this long wasn't a satisfactory excuse. The social worker informed us, "I couldn't tell you what Jeff's IQ is, or even if he's retarded, but I feel he'd be better off in his own district where he'd at least have a chance to make some friends. Talk to the psychologist who placed him here."

We went to see her, and when we left her office Bobby said, "She talked in circles. I'm not even sure what she was trying to tell us."

We informed her Jeff would remain at home rather than return to BOCES, and then she agreed to bring him back to Islip and put him in the retarded class there. I didn't like her suggestion and continued to grope for a way out, like a blind person in an unfamiliar place.

◆　　　◆　　　◆

Bobby and I wanted to do something special for Jeff's eighteenth birthday, a milestone, a miracle. Never again would his birthdays be days of depression for me. Each additional year was a bonus.

We planned a colossal surprise party, rented a hall, had it catered so Jeff wouldn't get suspicious, and split the cost between us, our gift to Jeff. The Suffolk Royals were among the seventy-five guests invited. The day of the party Liz and I told Jeff were going shopping so we could sneak to the hall to decorate. Streamers, balloons, Royal colors: orange and black, everywhere, yellow mums, centerpieces on round white clothed tables, and a sheet cake, hockey players on top.

That evening Jeff dressed in his suit with his birth certificate in his jacket pocket, thought he was going out drinking with Bobby and his friends at a local bar, the legal age for drinking was still eighteen then. Bobby lifted him into his car, putting the folded wheelchair in the trunk, and as soon as they pulled out of the driveway Liz and I quickly changed into our party clothes, loaded Jeff's motorized chair in the van and sped to the hall, to find guests already arriving.

Would Jeff give Bobby and Charlie an argument when they brought him to the hall? Knowing Jeff, he'd volunteer to wait in the car rather than have them carry him up the long flight of stairs. But somehow they convinced him, and as they wheeled him through the doors the blood drained from his face when he was confronted by so many people, relatives, neighbors, Bobby's friends, the hockey team, some of the players' parents and girlfriends, and even Jeff's special ed teacher from his elementary days

Jeff was overwhelmed with the gifts; shirts, cologne, a down vest to wear to games, a ceramic mug designed and made by Liz with the Suffolk Royals emblem on it and the most impressive gift from the team, a jersey with his name on it just like the players'. Jeff was ecstatic.

The only thing to mar that night was when I learned his elementary teacher felt he never belonged in her special class, and the teachers in the junior high had wanted him to remain that second year so they could work with him.

If only I had known back then

40

BATTLES

After Jeff's party and much deliberation I took the first step toward getting Jeff into regular classes. A re-evaluation was set up by the Muscular Dystrophy Association at Adelphi University in Garden City. I didn't care how his IQ compared with others his age, which was what had been thrown at me whenever I asked questions. I just wanted to know if he had enough intelligence to do the work required.

Bobby felt I hadn't been wise in taking Jeff to a hockey game the night before he was tested, he was tired and might have done better if he'd been well rested, but the game was important to him too.

I was elated when his test scores were above the retarded range, but the psychologist at Adelphi upset me with such remarks as, "There's an underlying depression," *Strange no one else had ever felt he was depressed, though he certainly had reason to be.* "Jeff is dismayed and astounded by the unrealistic goals his mother has set for him." (A statement in the report.) *There was nothing Jeff wanted more than to be treated normally. For years his homemade cards to me on birthdays and holidays carried the same message,* "I love you because you treat me like a person."

The psychologist added other comments like, "I feel the change to regular classes after so many years in special education would be too frustrating," and "He will be at the bottom of his class."

She did succeed in frightening me though, the last thing I wanted to do was harm him. Since he was already back in the high school, and the psychologist agreed to let him take part in three regular classes Jeff and I were satisfied, at least temporarily.

◆   ◆   ◆

Our new van arrived just before Jeff's eighteenth birthday and Bobby moved the hydraulic lift from the old van to the new. It's ironic I thought, Bill was the one who always wanted a brand new car; something that meant nothing to me. What was the sense of it when the payments would've gobbled up any money we might have had to go any place in it. Now I would be driving a new one.

As the holidays approached we began planning a trip to Florida instead of trying to make Christmas like the ones in the past. We—Bobby, Liz and I thought a visit to Disney and a short stay with Billy would be a good idea.

Again I worried, was I spending money foolishly?

Bobby did the driving, we registered in a motel and spent the next two days at Disney, Christmas Eve and Christmas. The immense tree in the village square, decorations everywhere, and the festive feeling in the air reminded us it was Christmas, but it was so different than any we'd experienced its uniqueness brought no anguish.

◆   ◆   ◆

The next months were anything but easy for Jeff and me. He was unsure, anxious, especially over exams, and I was afraid I _was_ expecting too much from him. But when he discovered he wasn't at the bottom of the class as had been predicted he began to relax and enjoy school more than he ever had.

The Royals were doing well, leading in points, and there was a good chance they'd be champions this year, which helped boost Jeff's morale.

On February 3rd, Liz's sixteenth birthday there was a game in Jersey, so we took along a birthday cake to share with the team after the game.

As the bus left Superior I noticed the driver glancing nervously at his feet. Was something wrong? I wondered. As we traveled along the Expressway he appeared concerned with the way the bus was shifting. We had just crossed to the Jersey side of the George Washington bridge when the bus ground to a halt and refused to start again.

A great deal of discussion followed between Norm, the other fathers and the bus driver. With a two-way radio the driver contacted the bus company and was promised another would be sent. We waited for what seemed hours. The bus grew cooler, outside it was dark and windy. Cars, buses and trucks whizzed by. No one dared leave the bus even though we weren't far from the rink. After about an hour I asked Liz if she wanted to cut her cake there on the bus.

"Sure, why not?" was her reply.

And so we cerebrated her birthday there on the bus.

"Not every girl gets to have a sweet-sixteen party with this many guys." she said laughing.

We never did get to game.

◆　　　◆　　　◆

At the last regular season game, about three weeks before the national championships, the Royals played the Essex New Jersey team. As soon as Liz finished practicing we flew home to pick up Bobby and Jeff, then to Superior for the bus, which shook with anticipation. The game proved an easy one, the Royals leading eleven to nothing in the third period. About forty seconds before the final buzzer a puck skittered past all-star goalie Frank DeMayo, spoiling his shut-out. There was some disappointment, but the victory was theirs

The Essex players had been testy, and fights were prevalent during the game, and when another broke out after the goal the officials called an end to the game. The teams lined up at center ice for the traditional handshake, and still another battle erupted.

Jeff, sitting hear the boards was yelling angrily at the Essex players for being such poor losers.

The players began to file off the ice, and suddenly there was more yelling and fists flying, and for a minute I lost sight of Jeff as he was swallowed up by the pushing, cursing mob. I turned as I felt a hand on my shoulder and found the worried face of one of the fathers, "Your son had been hurt. They've called an ambulance."

Heart thudding wildly, *"Jeff was hurt"* Then I spied him hollering by the glass. The man must have meant Bobby. Throwing caution to the wind I rushed into the milling crowd, and saw someone lying in a pool of blood. Though he was built like Bobby, with the same shade of dirty blond hair, I knew from the clothes it wasn't him. I turned back to where I'd left Jeff, shaking with relief.

Liz fought her way to me, "Are you crazy! You could have gotten hurt."

The police arrived, order was restored, but it was quite some time before we were all on the bus and headed home. Although the game had been won, the mood on the bus was one of defeat.

41

TRUE CHAMPIONS

While the other teams were preparing for Nationals by playing exhibition games, the Royals were only allowed to practice. They had been blamed for the unfortunate event at Essex, even though it had been a Jersey fan who had thrown the first punch.

For the next couple of weeks rumors flew, of suspensions and even the possibility of not allowing the Royals to participate in Nationals. When it finally was decided they could, several key players were barred and injuries had claimed a few more. The team's spirit was low, only time would tell how well they would do.

Bobby drove us to Jersey in the van and, we stayed in the same motel as the team and their families.

The Royals played well enough to advance to the semi-finals where they faced the same Essex team. The game was a complete fiasco, the Royals had no spark, and Essex beat them easily, ending their season. "Norm, is it all right if I go in the locker room?" Jeff asked the coach sadly, after the players came off the ice. A few minutes later he returned and was strangely quiet during the ride back to the motel.

Two players came to our room, "Come on Jeff. We're taking you upstairs to a party. There's no elevator, but we can carry you in your chair."

"Let me switch him to the other wheelchair, it's much lighter," I offered.

Liz and I followed them, found most of the players congregated in one room. I asked Jeff if he wanted a drink from the bar.

"A rum and coke," he ordered.

I went downstairs deciding not to return right away, knowing just being with the guys meant more than any drink.

Some of the parents were sitting in the dining room and invited me to join them. About forty-five minutes later the sister of one of the players burst in, "Mrs. E., Jeff's stuck upstairs, and we can't find Bobby to help get him down."

Along with a couple of the fathers I dashed up to find Jeff sitting there helplessly. The men carried him down, and I asked, "Would you like to go into the bar? Everyone seems to have ended out in there."

As we entered the dimly lit bar crowded with the players and their families Mr. Pavese came over to us and asked, "What would you like Jeff?"

"A rum and coke, I guess."

Mr. Pavese ordered the drink and set it on a small table near Jeff, while I fished in my pocketbook for a straw.

"Mom, what time is it?"

I placed my arm near the light so I could see my watch. "Twenty after two."

"It couldn't be", he said in disbelief.

"The game didn't end till 11:30, and it was after twelve when we got back here," I added.

"I don't believe you."

I turned to Mr. Pavese, "What time do you have?"

He showed Jeff his watch which read two twenty-five.

Fear tugged at me. Something was wrong. Jeff never acted like this before. Alcohol usually did bring his frustrations to the surface, but he hadn't even tasted his drink.

"Jeff, let's go back to our room. What you need is some sleep." I pushed his chair down the hall to the room, but things continued to worsen.

"Why are you doing this to me?" he demanded, tears streaming down his face, and the more I tried to reason with him the more distraught he got.

"Let me get you into bed. You'll feel better in the morning."

"I don't want to go to bed. If I go to sleep I won't wake up again. What's wrong with me?" he implored.

"You have Muscular Dystrophy, you know that. You just had your annual checkup, and everything was fine," I tried to reassure him.

"What did the doctor tell you? He found something wrong, didn't he? I'm dying."

This can't be happening. What should I do? I've read of people dying just because they believed they were. I need help! Call Norm's room, Bobby said he'd be there. With trembling hands I dialed, Norm's voice came over the wire.

"Is Bobby there? It's Mrs. E," trying to keep the panic from my voice.

"No, but I'll find him for you."

That was the extent of our conversation, but within minutes Bobby, Norm and Frank DeMayo were there.

"Something's wrong with Jeff. I can't talk to him, he won't listen. He thinks he's dying. I'm so scared."

They got Jeff into bed and stood talking to him. Word spread quickly through the motel, "Something's wrong with Jeff." The room began filling with players and parents.

Someone took my arm and led me to another room. Tears gushed from my eyes. I'd never felt so desolate. Comforting words, and an arm around my shoulders, whose I wasn't even aware of. Moments, an hour? The door opened. "He's all right now. He wants to see you before he goes to sleep."

◆   ◆   ◆

"He just reached bottom emotionally. He'll be okay," Norm assured me after Jeff dozed off.

There had been so much; it was just a year since his father's death, the battle with the school, the tests at Adelphi, the fear of failing in school, the trouble at Essex and his physical. Because the doctor had talked to me, not him, he felt we were hiding something. The loss to Essex had been the final blow. Sitting stranded at the top of those stairs, powerless, for how long? All those things probably racing through his mind.

The next morning he was himself again, just fatigued. No mention was made of the events of the night before. Bobby was offered a ride home that morning, but I stayed, feeling it important since it was what Jeff wanted. He cheered on the Los Angles team, but they too fell to Essex.I left there feeling Essex may have won the trophy, but the true champions to me, were the Royals.

42

AN INTRODUCTION

Liz's move to Racquet N Rink opened a new chapter in Jeff's life; it was there the New York Islanders practiced.

One day when Liz was skating, and Jeff had no school he went with us to the rink. While Liz practiced Jeff and I went to watch the Islanders scrimmaging on one of the other ice surfaces.

Al Arbour, the coach was standing near the boards watching the action so I approached him and introduced him to Jeff, "Jeff watches all your games on TV. And the first thing he turns to in the newspaper is the sports section to see what is written about the game."

Al then introduced him to some of the players, Bobby Bourne, Clark Gillies and Bobby Nystrom. At the time the players were a sea of faces to me, even their numbers meant nothing.

"There's John Tonelli, he's new. Doesn't he look great! There's another new player, Mike Bossy, but he's not practicing yet. He pulled a muscle or something."

To complete the day, Mr. Ahrens, Bommer's father from our Royal days, now rink manager at Racquet, went into the locker room and returned with an autographed hockey stick.

After that day whenever Jeff had no school, and knew the Islanders were there, he was ready to go.

He continued working very hard in school, and whenever he could did additional work for extra credit. He was determined to prove he was now where he belonged. It was hard not to berate myself for not doing something years earlier about his school situation.

His diligence paid off, and when the school year ended he'd managed to squeeze by, even though his final grades weren't very high. He was satisfied but exhausted.

When school was over we began pulling together our plans for another carnival. Donations had been pouring in for months.

◆   ◆   ◆

Now Jeff could identify all the Islanders, in uniform or street clothes, and the players were beginning to remember him.

Mr. Ahrens, besides managing the rink was a timekeeper for the Islander home games, and when his season tickets weren't being used he'd offer them to us. So we began going whenever we could to the games at the coliseum. One day while at the rink I talked to Bobby Nystrom about our carnivals, and he volunteered, along with Michael Bergeron to put in an appearance.

◆   ◆   ◆

A couple of weeks before the carnival Jeff called me from home, his voice brimming with excitement, "Mom, guess who called? Tommy Holmes from the Mets. I can't believe it, he's coming to the carnival too. Two Islanders and Tommy Holmes. Wow!"

He explained when we returned home that Tommy Holmes had set the record for most consecutive hits in the National League in 1945, and now Pete Rose of the Cincinnati Reds was closing in on that record. I had mailed our usual request for a donations, and along with some free tickets, Tommy Holmes was coming too. I spent hours painting a mammoth Islander emblem to use as a backdrop for taking pictures with the hockey players, Liz had put together another swim show, and the spook house, started early with Pete' s help was set.

We'd gotten a large shipment of florescent paint from the DayGlo Company, poster paints, pints and gallons of enamel, Horizan Blue,

Magenta, Neon Red, Lightning Yellow and Aurora Pink. Everything glowed brightly, backdrops made from wooden crates obtained at Fairchilds, posters and special effects in the spook house.

As you entered the garage eerie music drifted from a keyboard, a bloody detached hand resting on the keys. Blood, neon red, glowing from a concealed "black" light, an over-sized green and yellow crab, eyes glinting in the semi-darkness, peered menacingly from one corner, there were spiders on webs of string, dangling from the ceiling just low enough to brush the heads of visitors trying to decipher what strange substance they were wading through on the floor, and dim lights illuminating the borrowed coffin to reveal the black clad form reposing there, pasty white face with dark circles making the eyes appear sunken, ready to spring at anyone trying to squeeze by.

Liz made a monstrous cardboard shark that stood as high as the pool slide, to carry out the theme of the water show, <u>Jaws.</u> A smaller shark with an opening cut where the mouth was, made an excellent frame for picture taking.

The weatherman predicted showers. Only once before did we have to postpone a carnival, but late that night as we were putting the finishing touches on everything, a few drops began to fall. With sheets of plastic we covered everything we thought might be damaged by it, and instead of the youngsters sleeping outside they bedded down on the living room floor, amidst the mountains of prizes.

My sister Peggy and her family arrived, and we sat drinking coffee, watching the deluge. By ten o'clock we decided even if the rain stopped everything would be too wet. Roads were flooded so badly in some places they were impassable.

The phone rang unremittingly, "Should we come?" "Is there going to be a carnival?"

We told the callers we'd postponed it till the following weekend, and then Bobby Nostrum called, ready to start for our house. He sounded as disappointed as we felt when I told him of our decision. Because he was scheduled to appear at another charity event that next weekend he couldn't come. But Michael Bergeron's presence gave us a chance to use the emblem, and Tommy Holmes attracted many people.

We had another great carnival, topping the $2000. mark once more, but it was to be our last. There were too many things to be taken care of, and the first job Liz and I tackled was to paint the outside of the house. Because of my fear of heights, Liz did the top half and I, the bottom.

◆　　　◆　　　◆

A card arrived in the mail instructing Jeff to report to school one summer's day for yearbook pictures, and we learned the special class was being graduated the following June, just a social thing, I was told. Those students would receive a certificate of attendance, meaning nothing more than they'd spent twelve years in school. They were free to return that fall, since by law the school was obligated to keep them until they were twenty-one.

"I don't want to graduate like that. I want a real diploma," stated Jeff angrily.

I consulted with his teachers to see if they felt he could do regular class work, and they were positive with hard work and some help in areas where he was weak he certainly had as good a chance as anyone.

When I informed the psychologist of my intent to keep Jeff in regular classes with a diploma as his goal she told me, with obvious perturbation behind her words, "You'll have to request an impartial hearing."

The patient coordinator and a psychologist working with MDA felt their presence at the hearing might help, and they convinced me to turn the Adelphi report from the previous year over to the school psychologist, saying it was not as damaging as I feared. Still intimidated, I waited till just before the meeting to do so. All the psychologist knew about it was what I'd told her; Jeff had tested above the retarded range.

Expecting a bitter battle I was stunned when she announced Jeff had been retested and was no longer retarded. Now that I know more about the education laws there never was an impartial hearing, but back then it was all so new. He was told he had to earn eighteen credits, pass all competency tests, all without any extra help from the school. I felt she wanted him to fail.

In her eyes Jeff was no longer considered handicapped, and I was removed from the committee, even though I now felt I'd be more of asset. As another parent coming before the committee I would have felt reassured knowing someone there understood my feelings about my child, and that there was hope that eventually their child might be placed back with normal children.

After the first elation wore off it began to bother me that Jeff had so much to do in so little time. He'd gotten no credit for all those years in BOCES or for the three regular classes he'd passed. I wrote a letter to Charlotte Roth, the State Advocate for the Handicapped. "Wasn't he in a wheelchair? Didn't that make him disabled?" she asked.

After talking to the school psychologist, Charlotte said, "Call her and tell her you want Jeff labeled physically handicapped."

But when I did the psychologist balked, "Why not label him "learning disabled" instead?" was her suggestion.

But when I persisted she finally said, "I'll get in touch with the high school and see what they have to offer."

An appointment was set up between the assistant principal, the guidance counselor, the psychologist and myself. At this meeting I was offered all the extra help Jeff needed and physical therapy in place of the required gym program. A complete schedule for his remaining years in school were laid out with a diploma as the goal. He was to attend summer school at the school's expense to make up ninth grade work he'd never had, and I didn't understand why he was suddenly getting all this, but I didn't really care about the reasons.

Without Betty and Carol from Muscular Dystrophy, and Rick, Jeff's physical therapist standing behind and encouraging me I wouldn't have gotten through this time of complete emotional turmoil.

◆   ◆   ◆

Rick had been coming to "stretch" Jeff for almost a year when I attended my thirty-year class reunion. He came the next day to work with Jeff in the pool, and as usual I sat on the pool edge chatting. "I went to my class reunion last night. It was strange seeing so many people I hadn't seen since graduation. They gave us pins with our yearbook pictures and names on them so you would know who was who. I was amazed at how much more the men have changed than the women."

"That's funny. My parents went to theirs' last night too," he exclaimed.

"What school did they graduate from?"

"Huntington High"

"So did I."

"My mother's name was Hansen, Marion."

"And your father's Charlie Johnson," I finished. I'd known his mother since grade school.

Jeff considered Rick a good friend and looked forward to his visits even though the stretching was painful, and Jeff and his cousin Eddie teased Rick by calling themselves his victims rather than his patients.

Weeks after learning about his parents Rick came to the house and asked, "Would you like to see a picture?" And there I was posing with my skirt pulled up revealing my knees, a picture that had earned me the nickname "Legs" when I was about fourteen.

◆   ◆   ◆

A big disappointment for Jeff that fall was the folding of the Suffolk Royals. Knowing how much he'd miss going to the games, and how much he enjoyed watching the Islanders on TV and at practice, I suggested buying season tickets. "You could buy your tickets with some of your savings, and I'll see if your brother will go halves with me. Then he can take you to some of the games."

The tickets were expensive, but when I thought of how much he'd come out of his shell since attending the games at Superior I felt it a worthwhile investment.

One afternoon a call came from Randy Alessi a former Royal player, who along with Chuck Samar and Glenn Lewis, his former line mates had gone to play for the New Hyde Park Arrows. "Would you come and watch us play?" Randy asked.

It lifted Jeff's spirits to know the players hadn't forgotten him, and we made quite a few trips to New Hyde Park to watch their games, besides going to see the Islanders.

Not long after Jeff had his season tickets he began the ritual with the Islanders as he had with the Royals, after each game we'd wait by the press gate for the players to come up from the locker room, and the glow on Jeff's face told me he'd found something to fill the void left by the loss of the Royals.

43

MORE LOSSES

That first season ended with the Islanders the regular season champions, but a bitter defeat by the New York Rangers knocked them out of the playoffs.

It was a difficult pill for the Islander fans to swallow, especially Jeff, but with high school on his list of priorities the loss didn't devastate him as badly as I feared it might, the experience at Nationals with the Royals never far from my mind.

Elsie, Bill's stepmother who'd been operated on for cancer the previous year died in March, and I lost a good friend who'd bolstered my sagging spirits many times over the years.

Jeff lost a friend too. I received a phone call one afternoon late in April just before Jeff and Liz returned home from school. "It's Bob Ahrens, I'm afraid I have some bad news. Randy Allessi died today."

My stunned reply, "My God, what happened?"

"He was lifting weights and something burst in his chest. He died in the hospital. I thought it better Jeff heard it from you."

I thanked him for calling and paced the floor trying to overcome my disbelief. Randy, so athletic, such a talented hockey player, with so much to live for. How would Jeff take the news? So many people were dying before Jeff.

Randy's mother and father were surprised but pleased to see Jeff and I at the wake. "Randy was so happy about being asked to attend two of the top colleges and play hockey for them. He'd lifted a couple of extra sets and afterwards complained of severe chest pains," his father explained to me.

Jeff had school the day of the funeral, and I didn't suggest he take time off to go.

◆   ◆   ◆

Jeff was concerned about his upcoming exams, and we both heaved a sigh of relief when he passed everything.

That summer was to be different than any we'd had before.

Before the summer session got under way at the rink we were asked if we'd like to have a skater from another state living with us. I was a little hesitant, but Liz pointed out it'd be like having a sister.

So one Sunday afternoon Renee's family brought her from Chicago. I was to drive the girls to and from the rink each day. Liz had also made friends with Linda, from Rhode Island, who wasn't happy with the family she was staying with, so Liz invited her to come and spend the remainder of the summer with us. The three of them skated, went to the movies and swam in the pool, including Jeff most of the time. He loved having them with us, thought Linda was pretty special, not the first time he'd displayed a normal interest in the opposite sex. His first crush had been on our neighbor Dawn, then there had been a roller skater. The most traumatic had been Lynn, the sister of a couple of Royal players. Although she was a couple of years older, he had his dream, one that was shattered one summer afternoon when she came to our house for a visit.

We, Liz, Jeff, Lynn and I were sitting by the pool talking when Bobby came home from work. It was immediately obvious she found Bobby attractive, not unusual for most girls when they met him. Lynn began flirting with Bobby and after some time hinted, "Is there any-where nearby where I could buy some cigarettes?"

Bobby quickly offered, "I'll drive you to the store."

I went inside to answer the phone and when I returned just Liz remained.

"Where's everyone?"

"Bobby took Lynn to get cigarettes, and I thought Jeff went inside. He was headed towards the ramp out front.

I walked around to the front of the house and found him sitting, head down. "It's this damn chair! I'm as good as he is, but because of this stupid chair girls just don' t bother with me."

I had never seen him so devastated, and realized his feelings for Lynn went a lot deeper than I'd imagined.

Later that night I cornered Bobby, "Why did you do that? Why did you encourage her?"

"Lynn needed cigarettes so I offered to take her, that's all."

"Do you know how much you hurt your brother?"

"She's too old for him anyway, and besides if it hadn't been me, it would have been someone else."

"But don't you see, that made it even worse."

◆   ◆   ◆

Jeff's shrinking bank account worried him, so at the suggestion of Charley, my niece's husband, we purchased carnations and roses from a wholesaler, which Jeff sold sitting in front of the yard, weather permitting. With the money he made he insisted on paying for the parking at the coliseum and treating me to a snack at the games.

Then during the summer skating session I made friends with Eileen Rufrano, one of the skating mothers, who with her husband ran a farm stand in Nassau County. They owned acreage in St. James where they grew most of their own produce, and she began dropping of tomatoes for Jeff to sell along with his flowers. When he got home from summer school, part of the program set up by the school, he'd sit outside with his radio till supper time.

For me it was a summer of constant running because the girls did not skate at the same times. It was a twenty minutes ride each way, and I'd take Renee to the rink early, come back to drive Jeff to school, at least for the first two weeks till a bus was obtained for him, then back to the rink with Liz and Linda.

That summer Liz passed her seventh figure test and made an attempt at her eighth. She had to take the seventh twice, it was the first time she hadn't passed a test on the first try, and the eighth would be her final one.

It was to be the last of the skating at Racquet N Rink. Fairchild owned the building and needed the space, forcing the rink to close down. The head pro, Peter Burrows, and Neil Rubin, Liz's pro, were going to Monsey, New York. Many of the skaters would follow them, but it was out of the question for us. Even though Bill had rigged up a system where Jeff could open the front door, and could still dial the phone I felt I couldn't go that far from home and leave him.

So Liz returned to Superior and began working with Lynn Alberi, one of the top figure pros. Practice time was scarce, and Liz went early in the morning before school. I'd drive her to meet one of the mothers who was taking her two daughters to Superior and then return home to finish getting Jeff ready for his bus, and after school I'd take her back for more practice.

In September her eighth test was scheduled in Port Washington, but one of the judges failed to show up so there were no tests. More were set for November, this time at Newbridge and again there weren't enough gold judges, the only ones qualified to judge an eighth. The same thing happened the following month. Would she ever get to take it?

In desperation Lynn arranged for Liz to travel by train to Philadelphia to stay with her parents, practice on Saturday in a nearby rink and test there on Sunday. I was to meet them late Saturday, and was very nervous about traveling on the train by myself, but couldn't miss this last test. Bobby was to drive me to the Babylon station on Saturday morning, and Lynn was to meet me with her parents' car.

When I woke that morning it was bitter cold, the ground clothed in a carpet of white. Bobby had moved out months earlier and agreed to take Jeff to the Islander game and then sleep at our house with him on Saturday night. I had a great time even though Liz didn't pass.

A month later in Port Washington she became a gold medalist. It had only taken her five years, in spite of the months of delays over the last test, and one of the judges comments was, "She has Olympic quality figures."

I wondered how far she might have gone if we'd had the finances to back her?

We left the twin rinks in high spirits, but as we drove along Northern State Parkway on our way to Superior a brief moment of sadness touched me, "It's too bad your father didn't see you complete you tests."

Her reply, "Mom, don't feel bad. I doubt if I'd have gotten this far if he was still alive."

"You're probably right, No sad thoughts, it's a day to celebrate."

After we left the parkway we stopped at a liquor store and bought a bottle of champagne to share with everyone at Superior. After drinking a cup Liz insisted I don a pair of ice skates and go on the ice with her. Not very sure of myself I stepped gingerly on the ice only to find myself sailing furiously around the rink between Liz and Kim, another young figure skater.

Following our celebration at the rink I drove home to prepare supper before Jeff and I left for the Islander game.

Before the game began Mr. Ahrens put an eight in each corner of the scoreboard in recognition of Liz's accomplishment.

By the time the game ended, and we were back home again I was at the point of exhaustion. I'd driven over one hundred and fifty miles that day.

44

A WIN AND A LOSS

When spring arrived Liz bought her first car, which meant my chauf-feuring days for her were over. I thought I would miss going to the rink, but found I had time for the bigger jobs around the house I'd been putting off, like painting ceilings and papering the kitchen.

Liz wanted to move into what had been Bobby's room, so we tore out the bunk beds, applied a large mural to the wall they'd occupied, papered, varnished the cabinets and wood-work, glued cork around one window and on a part of another wall, and carpeted the floor. We moved the chair that opened into a bed that I'd bought when Renee and Linda were staying with us into her room.

The tiny bedroom became the spare-catch-all room, for my sewing machine, the ironing board, everything not being used or on its way to the attic for storage.

Now I was driving Jeff to all Islander home games, usually twice a week and to practice when he didn't have school.

By the end of the season the Islanders were in fifth place, and in the first round of the playoffs they faced the Los Angeles Kings at home, beat them with a resounding eight to one victory, then lost to them in the second game. An overtime victory and a shutout in Los Angeles moved the Islanders into the quarterfinals against Boston.

That series was a brutal one, but again the Islanders were the win-ners.

They made it to the finals by beating Buffalo, the team who'd expected to win Stanley Cup.

Four more wins and the cup would be theirs.

They now faced the formidable Flyers who had put together a thirty-five game unbeaten streak during the regular season. At the end of the third period of the first game they were tied at three, and in overtime scored to give them the game.

But in game two, the Flyers came back with an eight to three victory. The Islanders won the next two at home to take a three to one lead in the series, the next game would be back at the Spectrum.

"Jeff, how would you like to go to Philly?"

"Do you think we could? But how can we get tickets?"

"Let me talk to one of the players. I'm sure you want to be there if they win the Cup."

We were waiting by the press gate, and the first player to climb the long flight of stairs was Stefan Persson who stopped to ask Jeff what he thought of the game.

"Stefan, I'd like to take Jeff to the game at the Spectrum. Do you think we could get a couple of tickets? He wants to be there if you win the Cup that night."

"Let me see what I can do."

◆   ◆   ◆

The phone rang the next afternoon, it was Stefan calling from Philadelphia, "I've got tickets for you and Jeff. See you in Philly tomorrow."

After thanking him I hung up the phone and began dancing around. "We're going! We're really going!" The problem of transportation was solved by another phone call, from Nickie Trottier, Bryan's wife, asking if we would like to join the wives and friends of the team on a bus to the game; we were to meet at the Fairchild airport near Racquet N Rink the next afternoon. It'd take several hours to reach the Spectrum. We'd never attended an Islander game in any other arena than the Coliseum, and it felt strange being surrounded by so many fans rooting for the opposing team.

Most fans were friendly, one commenting, "The Islander's will lose tonight, but they'll win at home. You'll see."

And so at five-forty on Saturday, May twenty-fourth in the year 1980 Jeff and I along with thousands of others witnessed the winning of the Islanders' first Stanley Cup at the Nassau Coliseum. I don't believe any fan suffered as much as I did that day and doubt anyone was happier than Jeff at the outcome. All the pain and tears of the past few years were erased that afternoon.

In the fall Jeff returned eager and relaxed for his last year of high school, and about half way through began talking about going on to college after graduation.

I consulted with his teachers, and found they felt he could do the work if he could manage physically. I tried to impress on him he would only be going to learn as much as he could. No degree was expected, there were too many places he was lacking, things he should have been taught but wasn't.

At Islander practice one day he mentioned his plans to Billy Smith. "You better not go away to school, you're our good luck," the Islander goalie informed him. There are no words to express what those words meant to him. After the Islanders' victory Jeff's confidence in himself increased by leaps and bounds. At school he even ran into people who blocked the hallway; an unheard of action before, and he talked more with the people who stopped to buy flowers. He still had a long way to go, but he'd taken a giant step.

When he found things difficult he blamed the school, especially the psychologist for what he felt she'd done to him. But my philosophy that something good comes from everything no matter how bad it seems at the time still held true. Would he still be fighting for his life if he wasn't faced with proving himself now? I wondered. His life certainly was not filled with dating, cars and a job like most young men his age.

45

GRADUATION

The year flew quickly by, and playoff time was upon us once again.

Jeff came home from school to announce, "Kenny died of a heart attack yesterday."

I looked at him incredulously, "But he was at the game Saturday. How did you find out?"

"Rick told me at school when he came to stretch me today."

Heart attacks happen suddenly, but Kenny, another MD victim was only twenty-three. I watched Jeff closely, he seemed calm and yet how frightened he must feel. It was exactly a year since Artie's death.

I wondered if I'd been wrong in not wanting Jeff to spend more time with these other victims? He night have had more close friends, but wouldn't he have suffered more each time one died?

The next evening Patti, from next door arrived as I was combing my hair in front of the bathroom mirror.

"Where are you going?" she asked.

"One of the boys with MD died, and he's being buried tomorrow. I'm going to the wake."

Jeff was coming down the hall towards us.

"Hey Jeff, are you going with your mom?"

"What do you think?" he snarled at her, then spun around and headed back to his room.

"I'm going to see if I can talk him out of going with me. He's really uptight."

"I'll call home and see if I can stay and keep him company till you get back. That is, if you want me to?" she offered.

"Sounds like a good idea. I'll tell him I'm tired and don't really feel like loading him in and out of the van. If he thinks he's staying home for my sake, he'll agree."

◆   ◆   ◆

The playoffs began, there was no fear this time. The Islanders eliminated the Toronto Maple Leafs, then Edmonton felt their sting, and a complete trouncing of the hated Rangers moved them into the finals against the Minnesota North Stars. They beat them in the first two games at home and the first game in Bloomington, then came back home to the Coliseum where they clinched their second Stanley Cup Championship, and again we were in the locker room to join in the celebration.

Mike Rivien, who worked with the players, spotted Jeff and yelled, "Follow me!"

He led Jeff and I out the door, across the hall to another room where the enormous silver cup stood. "Come on Jeff, how about a drink of champagne from the Stanley Cup?"

As Mike tipped the Cup, Jeff drank, and flashbulbs blazed, barely outshining the luminosity of Jeff's happy face.

◆   ◆   ◆

With the playoffs over the next big event was Jeff's senior prom.

He invited Cindy, who lived just around the corner. He'd met her through his sister the day of Cindy's graduation two years earlier. Liz had come home during Cindy's party to get Jeff, and after that Jeff called Cindy often. Cindy's father had a form of Muscular Dystrophy, not the same as Jeff, and he too became a good friend.

It was an exciting time for Jeff, I took him to be fitted for a tux and ordered flowers. Cindy was to drive them in my van. It wasn't a typical couple leaving for the Huntington Town House the night of the prom, and I watched her back nervously out of the driveway with mixed emotions; sad he couldn't do the driving but proud he had the guts to even go.

◆   ◆   ◆

Graduation day was here!

Pete newly graduated from the University of Georgia flew home to be here for Jeff's.

Pete, Liz and I drove with Jeff to the school on a gorgeous summer day, and while Pete and I sat side by side in the bleachers Liz went to find some of her friends.

"Did you think you'd ever see this day?" Pete asked.

"No, not really. These past few years have been especially rough on him. You don't know how many times I wondered if I <u>was</u> expecting too much. But you helped to get Jeff here too. You taught him and me so much over the years."

The strains of "Pomp and Circumstance" filled the gymnasium, and slowly the graduates filed in and took their places. The sound of Jeff's motor was muffled by the music but still all heads turned as he entered. His head high, he wheeled his chair to his designated spot.

After the usual speeches, the names of the students were called off, and they came forward to receive their diplomas.

"Kimberly Eskard."

"Greg Eden."

"Jeffrey Eldredge."

The whirring of his motor filled the silence that had settled over the gym, and all eyes were riveted on Jeff as he guided his chair to the foot of the podium, a hand reached down to place the diploma in his.

As he turned to go back to his place the spectators began applauding. The sound of clapping swelling louder and louder. The entire class stood, thundering their esteem, tears glistened on almost everyone's faces.

Jeff bowed his head to hide the tears that slipped out and trickled down.

But I stood dry-eyed watching, thinking, *even without knowing the whole story he'd won their hearts.*

And I thought *His cup truly runneth over.*

46

TESTED AGAIN

Months before Jeff's graduation from high school it was recommended by the psychologist at school that he contact OVR (Office of Vocational Rehabilitation) to see if they could be of any help to him once he was officially out of school.

"You'll have to have a psychological examination first," the counselor advised him when we kept our appointment at the OVR office, and we informed him Jeff wanted to go to college.

But as we drove home Jeff complained, "Do I have to take those damn tests again? I am really sick of them."

"I guess if we want their help you have no choice."

"They will probably tell me I should not go to college," he added in a disappointed tone.

"Let us just go along with them and see. It won't be the first time we have had to fight for what we wanted."

◆　　◆　　◆

I drove him to the OVR psychologist's office where once again he was put through a whole battery of tests. At our next visit before the psychologist could even give us the results Jeff blurted out, "I did not test retarded, did I?" fear evident in his voice.

"No, but why would you ask such a thing?" the psychologist wanted to know.

I explained what had happened with his schooling and was surprised to hear the psychologist say he had written a book on how to prevent such a situation from occurring, adding, "This happens too often. But as far as Jeff's case goes, I feel because of his unfortunate placement he has missed out on so much and would be better off going to Human Resources for some kind of vocational training. I am afraid college would be too difficult."

Jeff wasn't very happy when we left his office, and I told him, "Let us talk to the counselor at OVR again and tell her what you really want is a chance to learn. In other words you want to continue your education by attending college."

We revisited OVR but came away only after Jeff agreed to give Human Resources a trial.

47

A DREAM

What a happy celebration followed Jeff's graduation, proving me wrong in thinking anything could surpass his eighteenth birthday party. Family friends, neighbors, his special ed teacher from his elementary days, many from Superior Ice Rink, Bobby's friends who had watched him struggle over the years. And although the Islander players had all scattered back to their homes for the summer, cards came from many of them, even one from Stefan Person in Sweden.

Everyone who was at the high school graduation was talking about the standing ovation he got. Days afterwards I heard stories about it from people who did not know I was related to him.

A few weeks after graduation be began attending Human Resources, leaving in the morning by bus and not returning home again till late in the afternoon. It was a long hot ride making him tired and irritable, and left little time for him to swim and even less time to sell his flowers and tomatoes.

He had already been accepted by a couple of colleges and was assured financial help. College was his dream, his mind had already been made up, and after a few days he refused to go back to Human Resources.

We returned to OVR and explained that Human Resources just was not what he wanted. Reluctantly his counselor promised to obtain enough money to pay for his books and a bus to transport him to and from school, emphasizing, "It is only a trial."

◆   ◆   ◆

He signed up for Accounting and Business Math, the only two courses he was familiar with from high school, and we informed the counselor, "There is the possibility that he can eventually go to work for his brother who has his own accounting office.

With his schooling settled for the fall we relaxed. I put Jeff's carnations in black plastic buckets filled with water in front of our fence with the umbrella from our picnic table to shade them, and when he had roses we kept them in the refrigerator in the house until he had a customer who wanted them. When he had tomatoes I would put them on a small folding table next to his portable TV. He kept his change in a small plastic box on his lap. He had many "regulars", and I marveled at the change that occurred in him since he first began his flower business. Now he chatted, unselfconsciously with those who stopped, no longer sitting there silently while they decided what they wanted. Gone was the painful shyness, and the obvious discomfort he'd always displayed, ever fearful someone would think, "He's retarded."

When the weather was really hot he spent less time selling and more time in the pool. His progress in the water slowed so much he could no longer "swim" lap after lap. A couple of times slowly back and forth was all he had the strength for now. He'd lost so much over the years, but never the will to keep going, making the most of every day

One afternoon as I sat on the coping watching him in the water, Bobby's car pulled in the driveway. He'd been living with his girlfriend Cindy, a move that had upset me but I had learned to live with it. Bobby spotted me by the pool, came out and announced, "Mom, I've got a surprise for you. Cindy and I are getting married, and Cindy wants to know if you would like to make the dresses for the girls in the wedding party?"

"I'd love to. How many will there be? And when is the big day? I asked excitedly and was little stunned when he said the wedding would be in five weeks, wondering if I could get them done in that short period of time. Cindy found a pattern and got each girl's measurements. There was to be Liz, Karen, the wife of one of Bobby's best friends, a girlfriend of Cindy's, all wearing yellow. Cindy' sister Lea, her maid of honor, would wear green.

Bobby drove Cindy and I to the South Shore Mall, and in the material store Cindy selected flowered chiffon-like fabric and wide satin ribbon for sashes. Because of the sheerness of the material slips had to be made also. For the next few weeks every free minute I had was spent at my sewing machine. I sighed with relief when the last hem was sewn and felt a glow of pride when I saw how pretty they all looked in the dresses.

Jeff was to be Bobby's best man, an honor that brought that Cheshire-cat smirk to his face. Dressed in his brown tux, he looked like a young Abe Lincoln with his head of ebony hair and the dark beard framing his face. A beard with a story behind it.

Many of the Islanders grew beards for the playoffs, supposedly it brought them good luck, and when the regular season ended John Tonelli asked Jeff if he was going to grow one too. I had been trying for months to convince him not to shave, with an ulterior motive. It would mean one less job that I had to do every morning. One word from John was all it took, and the beard became a permanent part of him for the next several years.

◆   ◆   ◆

The ushers for Bobby's wedding were his friends, both named Charlie. One we'd nicknamed "Ski" Charlie because we first met him when he won a pair of skis at one of our MD carnivals, and the name had stuck. The other Charlie we called "Crazy" Charlie because you never knew what stunt he'd pull next—"moon" someone, or dash into the street in his under shorts. Then there was Tommy, an old friend from the days when Bobby worked in the skate room at the roller rink, and Kenny, who belonged to the ambulance corp. with Bobby.

The reception was held in the same hall where we'd had Jeff's eighteenth birthday party. I'd gone shopping for a dress for myself and found a "dream". Pink, floor length, spaghetti straps, the bodice lace over polyester, a narrow pink ribbon for a sash and skirt pleated chiffon over polyester. When I put it on I felt like a prom queen.

I had been very upset when Bobby and Cindy had first moved in together, in those days it wasn't as common as it was to become, and it went against everything I'd been brought up to believe. Combined with the fear I couldn't cope with everything by myself since his father's death it had been a difficult time for me. Marriage hadn't done much to bolster my self-esteem, and I wasn't sure I was capable of keeping the house running smoothly. Bill had never "allowed" me to do anything but paint. If he was wall papering for instance, I was supposed to stand and watch, and keep the table free from wallpaper paste. Whether there were unconscious motives about Bobby's move in with Cindy they weren't that clear to me then. I just knew I was terrified to have full responsibility for Jeff and the house.

Determined not to dampen the festivities on their wedding day, I found myself having a really wonderful time.

48

SURPRISE!

Following the reception we were all to meet at Bobby and Cindy's house, about five minutes away from ours. No honeymoon was planned. They had gone on a cruise earlier. Cindy's mother and father had come up from Florida for the wedding and were to spend the week.

I loaded Jeff in the van first, and then all the leftover food was added. Dotty sat next to Jeff on one of the seats in the back, I sat opposite holding the remainder of the wedding cake and trying to make sure the rest of the food remained on the seat next to me. Liz had insisted on driving, and as we neared the traffic light on the corner of Montauk Highway and Brentwood Road it turned red. Forgetting the van was an automatic and not a shift like her car Liz jammed on the brakes thinking it was her clutch, and the van halted with a tremendous jolt. Dotty slid off the seat onto the floor on top of the rolls, which had spilled from the bags, cold cuts, rained down on her, the cake slipped to the floor from my lap as I tried to prevent everything else from following, leaving a smear of white icing as it came to rest against the van door. After Dotty assured us she wasn't hurt, gales of laughter shook the van until we reached our destination.

Cindy was able to save most of the food and cake, but it would be months before the last of the icing was finally eradicated from the van. Just when we thought we had it all, more would turn up.

Before Jeff, Dotty and I drove home Cindy's mother spread out the food we'd salvaged and we all ate again. Liz had left with some friends.

A few days later we all got together for a barbecue at our house before we drove to Yonkers Raceway to see harness racing. Jeff bet two dollars on a horse, winning $119. The man at the payoff window remarked, "It's not often a fifty to one shot comes in."

The wedding was the highlight of that summer, but Jeff's entrance into college that fall was constantly on my mind.

September was soon upon us and Jeff began his first semester at Suffolk Community College in Brentwood. A bus would pick him up in the morning and bring him back when his classes were over. It proved a difficult time for him but he refused to admit defeat. I watched him struggle but was thankful for the closeness that had developed with the Islanders, which kept his spirits up.

The Islanders were scheduled to play a home game on Thanksgiving Day that fall, the first one on a holiday since we'd purchased our first season tickets, so we had our turkey dinner early in the afternoon. Jeff and I left the house at six, even though the game wouldn't begin until eight. We had to be there for warm ups. I told people teasingly, "We're the first ones here and the last to leave," which wasn't too far from the truth.

Liz and her girlfriend Karen were coming later. Hair had to be washed, blown dry, and makeup applied.

I sat behind Jeff in our usual spot waiting for the team to come out on the ice. The Islanders were out first, and I checked to see what players were missing, who would be "scratched" from the game. Then my eyes shifted to the other end of the ice. With excited disbelief I almost screamed at Jeff, "Jeff, look! Look at number thirty-five on the Blues. It's Jimmy, Jimmy Pavese."

"Where?"

"Right in front of Mr. Ahrens." (the timekeeper)

"Wow! It is. It's really him."

I felt a creeping sensation as the goose bumps formed on my arms. It isn't often you see someone you'd followed as a kid in junior hockey make it into the National Hockey League. Jimmy had played for the

Suffolk Royals, the team that had introduced us to the game. His father along with Coach Norm Ryder had carried Jeff on and off the team bus when we'd traveled with them to their away games.

After the game standing by the press gate, "Mom, look there's Jimmy's mom," exclaimed Liz.

There was much embracing, and I congratulated his mother, aunt, and grandmother, on Jimmy's success. Peter, Jimmy's younger brother, also a former Royal went over to speak to Jeff who waited by the barrier. Then Mr. Pavese himself came up the stairs from the locker room. When he spotted Jeff his eyes filled with tears and he laid a hand on Jeff's shoulder, struggling to speak. I was horrified when I realized it wasn't just the emotion that was getting in the way, Mr. Pavese had been operated on for cancer a few years earlier, he was learning to speak again and it took a tremendous effort to utter even a few words. Tears filled my eyes as I watched.

49

EDWARD

Although I knew Jeff was having some problems adjusting to college I didn't realize how troubled he really was. Finally he told me his accounting teacher suggested he drop the class and switch to a program of general studies. He seemed relieved when I assured him it was fine with me. "You're not there to get a degree, just to learn. Pick out what looks interesting and don't worry. You're not the only one who switches before he finishes his first year."

Unfortunately, OVR didn't feel the same way. I was advised since he didn't have a specific goal they would no longer help him in any way. I thought of the many students who went through several years of college before they made up their minds, but because he was disabled he wasn't allowed that freedom. Jeff and I were put in touch with a man who wanted us to fight them and an appeal was initiated for his funding to continue. He was expected to defend himself, but he hadn't gained enough confidence to go up against anything so threatening and the appeal eventually failed.

The semester ended and Christmas came and went. Ten days after, the phone jarred me from a sound sleep in the wee hours of the morning. It was my sister Jo who's son was also a victim of MD, informing me that Edward had lost his battle with MD.

What started out as a common cold, something greatly feared by those of us who knew how dangerous one could be, had taken it's toll on him.

◆   ◆   ◆

My mind flashed back to the previous April when Kenny had died at twenty-three from a heart attack just before the playoffs, and Jeff had predicted, "Edward is going to be next."

Rick had come to "stretch" Jeff, and afterwards I walked with him to his car on the pretext of getting the newspaper from the mailbox. "Jeff thinks Edward will be next. Please, tell me honestly how you think the two of them are doing?"

"Jeff and Edward will both be around for quite a long time yet," he assured me. Now all I could think of was how upset Rick must be. Jo had called him when she realized Edward was in trouble but he had gotten there too late to help.

◆   ◆   ◆

I dressed, than went into Jeff's room. There was no easy way to break the news. "Jeff, I have some bad news. Edward is gone. He died this morning."

"Oh, mom, how awful!"

And I wondered again, *What is he feeling?* "I'm going to Aunt Jo's as soon as you're all set. I think it might be too upsetting for her to see you today."

After I dressed Jeff, he ate his breakfast, I washed his face, combed his hair and helped him brush his teeth, then I got into the van and headed for the North Shore. Stopping at Bobby's house on the way to tell them what had happened.

The gas gauge on the van read below one quarter, but I kept putting off stopping for gas, and luckily made it to my sister's.

We sat, drank coffee, talked and cried. I kept expecting Edward to come wheeling into the room any minute. It was hard to believe we'd never see his cheerful face again. People came, the phone rang insistently as the day flew by. When the time came to head home my niece Vera sent her boyfriend for gas for the van. Aunt Jo, Vera and I stood giggling hysterically in the street as he poured enough gasoline to get me to the first gas station.

"The neighbors must think we're terrible," choked out Aunt Jo between fits of laughter. We hugged and as I climbed into the van I said, "Let me know what time Edward will be laid out. Call me if you need to talk. Would it be too painful to see Jeff?"

"No, you could have brought him today," was her answer.

As I drove home I thought, "*How will I take it when It's Jeff?*" He had already lived four years longer than the doctors had predicted that fateful day when he was just five and I'd first learned he had Muscular Dystrophy. The progress of the disease had been slow but relentless.

The next few days were spent running to the funeral home in Huntington, and then Edward was laid to rest out on the eastern end of Long Island. He was just nineteen, the same age as Liz.

Shortly after Jeff came down with a cold and fear filled my whole being. He didn't say, but it was obvious he was badly frightened too. He woke me many times during the night, something he'd never done before. Rick came and tried to reassure him, and as the cold subsided so did some of the terror.

Rick was badly shaken by Edward's death, blaming himself for not being able to prevent it.

"Don't you predict who is going to be next," he teasingly admonished Jeff.

I had lived with the fear of Jeff's death for so long, but never had it been as strong as it was now. I reaffirmed my vow to make every day as full for him as I possibly could.

50

A SUGGESTION

The spring semester began, and we notified OVR that Jeff would continue going to go college. Their reaction, "Your feelings regarding this case are that you are interested in attending a college program with no specific goal. We feel that is not realistic. Case closed."

Anger boiled in me. *Did we have to fight for everything? If Jeff wasn't disabled no one would object to him enrolling in a general studies program, hoping to find what he wanted to do.* His tuition was covered, and I decided I would drive him to school and pay for his books myself.

It didn't seem practical to run back and forth between home and campus so I sat in the van when the weather was warm, and when it got too chilly I would sit in the lounge reading, knitting or writing. I had done it for years with Liz with her skating, so now I would do it for Jeff. One accomplishment during that time was a christening outfit for Cindy and Bobby's first son who was born a few weeks after Edward's death.

Jeff still had a great deal of frustration to deal with. The fear of appearing retarded hung over him like an ominous cloud, making him hesitant about questioning things too much. I was more and more distressed over what his misplacement in school for all those years had done to him.

He enrolled in a computer course at my suggestion. He'd done well in typing in high school and enjoyed computer games. Because of his hesitation over asking questions he began to fall further and further behind the rest of the class. When I realized the problem was he wasn't going to the computer room to work on his own, I began going with

230 Cup Runneth Over

him hoping I could be of some help. But with my lack of computer knowledge I wasn't much help. By the end of the semester his computer teacher announced, "Anyone who receives a "D" in this course shouldn't think about continuing with computers."

Jeff was one of those students.

"Don't listen to him, he doesn't know you and your problems. If you want to try another language, go ahead. You know what's expected now and with another teacher you will probably do better."

Pre-registration time arrived at Suffolk, and Jeff and I went to see Judy Taxier, his counselor about his schedule. "Why don't you sign up for classes?" Judy asked me, "You sit here everyday anyway."

"I don't know," I said hesitantly. "It's been a long time since I finished high school."

"Take a schedule and look it over," she suggested.

At home I studied it thinking, *This is crazy. What would I take? Creative Writing? Why not?*

Jeff had signed up for a computer course in RPG programming

"Jeff, how about I take the same course? Then we could work together. Would you mind me being in the same class?"

"No, then you could take notes and help me with my coat."

So I settled on three classes. Writing, computers and a typing course. Returning to school thirty years after graduation from high school, now in my fifties wasn't the easiest thing I'd ever attempted. And so began a new life for me, one I was to thank OVR for. The old adage was proving true again, something that was to be a lifesaver for me came from their denial to give Jeff his chance.

51

SUCCESS

It would be an understatement to say that the first day of class I was terrified. I felt ancient with all those young men and women fresh out of high school, although there were a couple of "older" students, but they seemed so sure of themselves, not cowardly, like me.

The professor in the Creative Writing class introduced herself on that first day, passed out index cards for us to fill out with our names, addresses, etc. and a list of the English courses we'd already taken. After collecting the cards and glancing through them, Professor Celeste Berner stated. "Anyone who has not had previous college courses in English doesn't belong in here and should see me at the end of the class." Timidly I approached her desk when the class ended along with several other students. I hung back till everyone else had spoken to her and then advanced, "I really should not let you stay in this class. I'll make an exception but—" Her doubts did little to ease my fears.

As an assignment we were asked to bring in something we'd previously written. Some students brought poetry, others stories they'd written. I had a few short stories I'd done for a correspondence writing course I'd taken just after Bill's death but decided instead to give her a chapter from the beginning of this book which I'd worked on sporadically for several years. As time went by, Celeste and I became good friends and she enthusiastically encouraged me to work on the book as my project for that class. Up to that point I wondered if what I had written was of any interest to anyone. But Celeste and the class soon instilled the confidence I lacked. Before long I was handing in chapters regularly, which Celeste would make copies of and send home for the others to read and critique for the homework. When the semester ended the chapters had piled up, and when pre-registration arrived I again enrolled in her class. At that point I had no intention of going for a degree so it wasn't important what classes I took. Celeste and I often looked back in the next few years, at that first day in class and laughed.

The computer class also proved to be a success, especially for Jeff. We worked in the computer room on our programs and studied together, and when that semester ended Jeff had a B+ and I an A. We were both feeling pretty good about ourselves and it turned out to be a turning point for him. I can't say he never had any more doubts about himself or his abilities, but he came away feeling he really could learn and was eager for the next semester to begin. But first came the summer, one that proved to be an unforgettable one for Jeff.

52

MAGIC HARBOR

Liz was to spend the summer performing in an ice show in an amusement park in South Carolina. The park, Magic Harbor, featured a Ferris wheel, which had been shipped here from England, supposedly the highest one in the world, a log flume, a roller coaster, a puppet theater, a few games, and a variety of refreshment establishments. The skaters, of which there was a total of eight stayed in mobile homes owned by the park. There were four other girls besides Liz, three of whom she shared one mobile home with. The fifth, and the feature skater lived in another mobile home with her husband, the park manager. The remaining skaters were a comedy team from England, three males, called the Jackpots. Steve, Mackey and Rob. Liz had told them all about Jeff, and from what Liz had told us about them we felt like we already knew them.

For the first six weeks at the beginning of the summer Jeff worked for the Town of Islip Recreational Department, his first real job. We planned on driving to Magic Harbor late in August.

The long drive scared me and when we had trouble with the pool filter a few days before we were to leave I came close to canceling our trip. Without the filter the water would turn green. It seemed like an easy enough thing to buy and install a new one but I was sold the wrong fittings, which put me in such a state Bobby stepped in and told us not to worry he would have it fixed when we left.

We left early on a Friday afternoon, and I drove till darkness set in, and we were somewhere in Virginia. Luckily I had no idea I had to drive through the Delaware Tunnel or I would have stayed home for sure.

Both of us were exhausted, so we looked for a motel to spend the night. Though all we could find was a room with a queen sized bed we were so tired we would have been willing to sleep on the floor. Jeff had not been out of the van since we left New York. Everything had to be unloaded before I could get him out so we had even eaten in the van When we reached the motel I unloaded the hydraulic lift, pushed that into our room. Then using his manual wheelchair I loaded our luggage on that. When everything was safely in the room then I was able to get Jeff in his motorized chair out. We both fell asleep as soon as we were on the bed.

The next morning the process had to be reversed, before we could continue on our way. We should have arrived in Magic Harbor within another five or six hours, but instead it took us eleven. The weather was extremely hot, and after a few minutes of driving I noticed the temperature was inching up on the gauge on the dashboard in the van. Remembering something I'd once heard, "If your vehicle begins to overheat, turn off the air conditioning and turn on the heater to draw some of the heat from the engine." The van didn't have air conditioning so I proceeded to turn on the heater. It didn't take long for the van to become almost unbearably hot, making the two of us sweat profusely. When the temperature of the engine continued to rise we decided to stop under the next bridge to let it cool. So every fifteen minutes or so we would stop and sit for about twenty minutes. I was afraid if I stopped to have it looked at and the operator of the service station saw I was alone, more or less, he might charge some exorbitant amount to fix it. I just wanted to get to Magic Harbor.

So we left Virginia early that morning and arrived at our motel on the beach late that night. I had never felt so tired, and again the van had to be unloaded.

We drove to the park the next morning and were directed to the building where the skaters were half way through their first show of the day. We quietly found a place where I could sit with Jeff next to me in the wheelchair. They spotted us right away and using a segment of the show where they usually clowned around with the audience they came directly to greet us. Steve sat next to me giving me a big sloppy kiss on the cheek, leaving a red mark from his make-up on my face, and sitting so close with his wet costume I was soaked too. Then they jumped back on the ice and continued the show. We tried to be there for every one of their shows, and before long they made a game of changing little things in it to see if Jeff would notice, which he always did.

The Jackpots made Jeff feel like he was part of the show, something he had never experienced before. The entire week we were there it was like being at one big party. And before we left to return home they checked the van, flushing out the radiator and our trip back was uneventful.

Steve, Mackey and Rob promised they would visit us on Long Island when the park closed for the season and before their trip back home to England. They brought along two other Englishmen who helped run the show and stayed at our house for two maniacal weeks. Jeff and I were back in school but we managed to keep up with our homework and survive such craziness as we had never seen. They were two of the happiest weeks of Jeff' s life, every meal like a holiday dinner. We hated to see them go when it was time for them to fly back to England. They made us promise to come there and visit them sometime.

53

FEAR RETURNS

When Jeff returned to college in September there was a dramatic change in him. When I would meet him between classes he would be brimming with some choice bit of information he had just learned in his previous class. He was like a small child at Christmas who had just opened up a present he had dreamt about but never really thought he would get. He was lapping up knowledge like a thirsty pup. When he glowed, I did too. When I look back over those years at Suffolk I can still picture him motoring out of the music room, Cheshire-grin on that usually serious face uttering these words, "Did you know—?" And I would think, *Thank God I wasn't wrong. He belonged there. It was not a mistake.*

His self-confidence was growing steadily. Even further proof of that was when Gene made some remark at a hockey game that angered Jeff, now instead of turning to me to complain, he yelled at Gene. *This is great! How far he has come in the last few years.*

Another semester passed and Jeff continued to blossom. Then shortly after the New Year he caught a cold, and the terror I'd felt when Edward died returned. *"Its just a cold,"* I kept telling myself, *"He's weathered them before."*

I couldn't let him see how scared I was. I took his temperature, 99 degrees, only slightly above normal, but I called the doctor anyway. *Why take chances.*

Dr. Bernhardt had retired about six months earlier, and his replacement wanted to examine Jeff before prescribing any medication. The appointment was for 3:00 that afternoon. I had one class at college, thought about skipping it, then finally decided to go only to find it had been canceled. I drove back home and tried to study for a Spanish test I was having the next day while waiting for the time to leave for the doctor's.

Two forty-five rolled around and I helped Jeff into his jacket, putting his knitted Islander hat on his head, and drove him to the doctor's office. We sat in the waiting room watching tropical fish swim around in the tank. I refused to let myself think about Edward.

Once in the office the doctor took out Jeff's chart and remarked, "It's been ten years since you've been here."

"He goes to Stonybrook University Hospital for regular check-ups, and the only two times he needed a doctor, Dr. Bernhardt was off, and I had to call his stand-in." With an attempt at humor I didn't really feel, I added, "Jeff's been the healthiest invalid I know."

Dr. Ferguson checked Jeff's blood pressure, listened to his chest and took a culture from his throat. Jeff told him he was allergic to penicillin and the doctor wrote a prescription for Erythromycin, "I'll give you some samples so you can get started on the medication right away."

"What's that?" Jeff asked. "Its not a muscle relaxant, is it?" I knew from the question that Edward's death was on his mind. Edward had been on several medications at once just before he died, and one had been just that. That plus the fact that Edward's attending physician had been reluctant to sign the death certificate had disturbed me at the time. I wondered if he should have been given a muscle relaxant at all. But the doctor never gave a reason for his hesitation and finally did sign it.

Back home after taking one of the samples of antibiotic the doctor had given him, Jeff said, "I'll stay in my room. It's warmer in here. I feel kind of cold."

Fear churned up inside me again. I busied myself preparing steak, French fries and lima beans, which Jeff said sounded appetizing. When the food was ready we ate silently, and then Jeff returned to his room to watch the Ranger-Blackhawk hockey game. I cleared the table, stacked the dirty dishes in the dishwasher and tidied the kitchen. Jeff called from his room, "Mom, can I have a blanket to put over my legs? They're freezing."

As I went into my bedroom to get the afghan my mother had cro-cheted many years before, I scolded myself silently, *"He feels cold because of the fever."* The doctor's thermometer had registered 100.2. *"He'll be all right."*

But as the night wore on the fear mounted. The blanket didn't seem to help, and Jeff complained his arms were cold too.

I returned to studying my Spanish but found it almost impossible to concentrate. I finally closed my book and went back to watch the game with him.

"I'm going to bed right after the game ends," he informed me.

"You could get in bed now, and if you fall asleep I could wake you when its time for your medication."

"No, you know how hard it is to take anything when I'm in bed."

So I stretched myself out on his bed, raising the head section with the electric control. It had taken some psychology to convince him to let me ask MDA to order him a hospital bed months earlier, but once he had it he was pleased with the freedom it gave him. Now he could sit up in bed and watch TV, and with his remote control it also freed me to go to bed if I wanted while he was still watching.

"Mom, I have to blow again."

I tried not to show my annoyance over his constant demands, but the dread I was feeling increased my impatience. A fleeting thought streaked through my mind, and I reprimanded myself, *"How are you going to feel if he does not make it?"*

The Rangers were ahead by one, three to two, with only about seven minutes left in the third period.

"Damn, they had to get that last goal," Jeff cursed softly.

Then Chicago tied it again. A five minute overtime.

"My nose again."

As I held the handkerchief to his reddening nose I put my arm around his shoulders, "Poor Jeff, you look so sad. Red eyes, red nose."

Then terror stabbed a little deeper, "I feel so weak."

When Chicago scored the winning goal, ending the game, a smile sliced across his face.

After he took his medication, I slid him onto the bed, removed his shirt, shoes and socks and pulled his pants from his bent legs. After arranging the pillows between his left leg and the wall, and his right leg and his chair, placed the control for his bed on his chest and arranged the covers over his arms.

See you in the morning," I said in what I hoped was a cheerful voice and left him.

I poured myself a glass of brandy, hoping it would settle my jumping nerves. A question that had gnawed at me all day nagged even more persistently. *What do I tell his sister if she calls from Florida?* She had gone to join another ice skating show. *If I don't tell her Jeff's sick and something happens, will she understand? And if I do tell her won't she worry too much?*

I tossed and turned till I finally fell asleep. I woke to the patter of rain on the window. Brandy, our German Shepherd was stretched out across the foot of the bed and moved closer when she realized I was awake. I lay patting her gently, my mind filling with last night's fear. *What will I find? What if he's not breathing?*

I got slowly out of bed, pulling on my slippers and robe and stumbled through the dinette, the kitchen and down the hall. I hesitated for a brief second trying to steel myself for what I might find.

I stepped into his room and was greeted with one of his silly smirks which appeared whenever he accomplished something difficult.

54

A RETURN VISIT

Another summer approached and again Jeff was to work for the town for six weeks. During the fall and winter he had worked Friday nights and Saturday afternoons. Liz was going to Magic Harbor to skate in the show again, and we made our plans to drive down at the end of the summer. This time though a friend of Bobby's, Tommy Lee and one of Liz's girlfriends, Tina were going with us. I was thankful because I wasn't looking forward to that drive again.

Tommy had spent a lot of time at our house over the years, was in the process of a divorce, and had developed back problem. When he discovered swimming was good for it he spent as much time as he could in the pool. He had met the Jackpots the summer before when they had visited us and decided a trip to Magic Harbor was just what he needed.

So the four of us piled into the van and once more headed for South Carolina. Tina had placed a cheesecake I had baked for Mackey's birthday in the a cooler filled with ice cubes to keep it fresh. But by the time we reached Magic Harbor, the ice had melted and the cake was submerged. We managed to eat it after it had dried out a couple of hours. It was to be the first of many mishaps we experienced during our stay.

One afternoon as we were leaving for the Park from the motel, Jeff discovered he had a flat tire. He'd run over a tack just before we left home but we thought it was just low on air and stopped at a gas station to inflate it, hoping that was all it needed. Now it was flat again.

At Tina's suggestion we stopped at a drug store and bought a can of foam for flats. We returned to Magic Harbor and attempted to repair his tire. Tommy removed the cap from the valve on the can, and on the tire, following the directions screwed the end of the attached tube into the tire, set the can upright, removed the cap and pressed. Immediately the tire began to inflate.

"Oh, oh," uttered Tommy.

"What's wrong?" worried Jeff.

"The tires inflating all crooked."

Quickly Tommy began unscrewing the can, but foam continued to ooze from it, piling up like mountains of marshmallows. Tina and I burst into fits of laughter. Luckily Jeff couldn't see what was happening or he would have been even more upset. Tommy was covered with white blobs of foam, in his hair, on his arms, shoulders and face, making him look like an abominable snowman. He took the car key and pressed it against the valve, but foam continued to spurt out. When the can was finally empty and Tommy had cleaned off most of the foam we headed for the ice show. Tina and I walked behind trying to control our laughter as Jeff's wheel turned erratically, and Jeff continued to fret. After the show was over we went searching for a new tire to replace it.

After the new wheel was put on we all congregated at the British Pub, one of the concessions at the park. Everyone was drinking English Beer, a dark strong liquid that had Jeff doing figure eight's in the parking lot.

No one wanted to call it a night so we piled into our cars and drove to a local nightspot. When that one closed down we proceeded to a place that stayed open past two. It was located on the second floor of a building on what was called "the strip". We had just gotten settled at a table, everyone had ordered drinks, and I asked Tommy, "Do you have the keys to the van?" We had been taking turns doing the driving and I wasn't sure who had ended up with the keys. "No, I thought I gave them to you." was his answer.

When I couldn't locate them in my pocket book. "Maybe I left them in the van when I unloaded Jeff. I better go check."

"I'll go," offered Liz.

Within minutes she was back with a strange look on her face. She handed me the keys then headed back out again, and at my question, "What's wrong?:" shrugged her shoulders, saying only, "I'll be right back." Joannie, one of the girls from the ice show went with her. "Something's wrong. I'm going to see what's happening."

Jeff chimed in, "I'm coming too."

Back down to the parking lot we went to find Liz standing besides a police car. "What's going on? Did something happen to the van?"

Liz was arguing with the policeman about something, and even mild-mannered Joannie sounded extremely angry. When everything was sorted out we learned Liz had come down to find the van being hooked up to a tow truck. According to the policeman we were illegally parked. We had left the van in the only empty space we could find, a parking lot of a miniature golf range that was closed. There were many other cars parked there, including a van adjacent to us. What we didn't know was that on the other side of that van was a sign, "No Parking." Every time we passed that lot after that night we saw the same empty spot with the same van parked next to it, blocking the sign. We decided we had been set up. Having New York license plates did nothing to elicit any sympathetic feelings towards us. Liz had finally gotten the tow truck man to agree to unhook the van when she offered him thirty dollars. We figured it would have cost us at least that much and a lot of aggravation if she hadn't gone down when she did.

The greatest adventure though was a ride in a helicopter. For twenty-five dollars two people could go for a ride. Somehow Steve convinced Jeff to go up with him, a very courageous thing for Jeff to do considering a simple thing like sitting him on the edge of his bed and trying to help him get his balance or having someone besides me lift him from his chair to another spot was usually a major crisis. I was dumbfounded that he agreed to go.

After their ride Steve started teasing me. Even though I was deathly afraid of heights I couldn't let Jeff go back home and tell people he had done it but I was too scared. I imagine my fingerprints are still on the seat I was sitting in, I held on so tight. When the pilot flew out over the ocean I asked timidly, "Are you sure you have enough gas?"

For Jeff there was a couple of things that stood out more than anything else. Every-one went out of their way to include him in everything that was done, not in a condescending way but like he was an equal. And there was Tappie, one of the girls in the ice show, Jeff fell for in a big way. After we were back home he began calling her several times a week, just to see how she was.

Before we left for home we watched the ice show one last time and the Jackpots came down into the audience and carried Jeff in his wheelchair onto the ice so we could get pictures of everyone together. The end of a memorable week.

◆   ◆   ◆

Jeff and I continued school, and by spring of '86 it was evident that the unthinkable was going to happen, Jeff was going to graduate with a degree in General Studies. He was as unbelieving as I was. It had taken a total of five years to complete the requirements for at two-year degree, but we'd never expected him to make it in _any_ amount of time. He had worked very hard, met so many nice people, and loved almost everything about his time spent there.

Jeff's brother Billy flew up from Florida for the big day. Tommy agreed to pick him up at Laguardia Airport using my van, because his car was too small to accommodate Billy, his luggage and Tommy's girl-friend. Billy was arriving the night before the graduation exercises. Several hours after Tommy left I received a phone call informing me the van had died on the way, somewhere in Nassau County. As much as I hated to, I ran next door to Mr. Crawford, who owned a tow truck and after the usual scolding about why I let Tommy take the van, he agreed to go get them.

Once he realized how important the next day was for us, especially Jeff, he went out of his way to try to get the van repaired. In spite of his efforts we were unable to use the van and had to lift the extremely heavy motorized chair into Liz's Turismo hatchback. We got there in time for the ceremony, and tears streamed down Jeff's face when he was handed his diploma. Another miracle. And now even I began to wonder, *"Will he be one of the few exceptions that lives a long life in spite of Muscular Dystrophy?"*

55

PETE AND KRIS

Pete had worked for a year in Seattle, Washington, and on his return moved to New Hampshire where Kris, a girl he'd worked with was from, and they were planning their wedding. Jeff was asked to be in the wedding party. Afraid the van would give us trouble if I tried to make the six hour trip and wanting Jeff to fly on an airliner at least once in his life I convinced him we would go by plane.

The arrangements didn't prove to be easy though. First there was the problem of his chair. He preferred taking his own, but the airline said his batteries couldn't be flown because they might leak. So I called Pasco and inquired about special jell-filled ones I'd heard about. I was told they did not hold a charge very well, were very expensive and there could be a problem recharging them. We could have left his batteries at home and gotten new ones there, but I doubted I would be able to install them and didn't want to bother the other guests. It was finally worked out that the MD association in New Hampshire would loan him a chair. We tried to cover all eventualities. Pete even measured our lift for getting Jeff in and out of bed, to make sure it would fit under the bed at the hotel where we were staying. But getting his lift there proved to be another problem, and MD offered to loan us a lift also.

Liz drove us to the airport where Jeff was carried on the plane with a stretcher-like appliance and settled in his seat. On landing at Boston Airport we were met by friends of Pete who had a van equipped for wheelchairs for transporting two sons with the same affliction.

They drove us to the hotel, where we discovered one suitcase was missing, the one with Jeff's wallet in it. He usually carried it in his plastic caddie on his chair. After a few anxious minute it turned out it was left in the van and was soon returned to us.

After unpacking a few things I attempted to push the lift under the bed, but it wouldn't fit. I called the desk hoping they could in some way raise the bed but was informed there was no one in maintenance working because it was a weekend. Our problem was solved in a rather unique way, Pete's brothers each lifted a corner of the bed while I slipped a Bible underneath. We all had a good laugh wondering what the management must have thought after we checked out.

The wedding was followed by a large reception, but as much as Jeff enjoyed himself, he found it difficult to get comfortable in the strange chair. On the return flight his legs and back were both aching, and no matter what I did he was miserable. After landing I had to push him in his non-motorized chair through the airport. Because it was lower than his other chair his feet dragged unless I tipped it up on the back wheels. My arms grew tired and by the time I met Liz Jeff's shoes had fallen off several times, his socks were full of holes. I was exhausted, irritable, and just wanted to get home where everything was easier. I was glad we'd gone, happy Jeff had gotten a chance to fly but swore to myself only something as special as Pete's wedding would ever tempt me to make such a trip again.

Bobby and Cindy had sold their home on Long Island and moved to Florida the previous year, a move that had upset me very much. I was bothered more for Jeff's sake than mine. How he missed his two nephews. Neither of his brothers could understand why I didn't just hop a plane with Jeff and come and visit them. I refused to drive that far, and after the trip to New Hampshire I informed them if they wanted us to come, it was up to them to make all the arrangements. I wasn't about to put myself through that again.

56

MIQUEL

The next memorable event was the arrival of Miquel into our lives. Judy Crawford asked me one day if I would be willing to take in a friend who needed a place to stay. I agreed and one Saturday morning a van pulled up in front of the house, a man got out and a young Puerto Rican boy. My first reaction when I saw him was, *Oh, God, what did I get myself into?* My only association with anyone from Puerto Rico had been Bobby's "friends" at the roller rink, always fighting, constantly in trouble with the law, drugs, the whole business. I realize it is wrong to stereotype people, but I hadn't known any living locally that were the type you'd brag about as friends.

As it turned out Miquel was with us over two years and became as close as any family member. When he left to join the Navy I cried like he was one of my own sons. To Jeff he was a brother, a friend, and they spent many happy hours together.

He moved in shortly before Christmas. I bought him his first Christmas stocking, and almost every dish I prepared in the first months were new to him. He teased me constantly about rice and beans, a favorite food back home. I even bought a Puerto Rican cookbook but never did get around to experimenting with it. After being with us for several months he got a job working in Grummans, a step up for him, but it meant he had less time to spend with us. He added so much to Jeff's life in the years he was with us, and were all saddened to see him go. We kept in touch through the Gulf war, the last letter I received was just before he was to return home, and then nothing. Although I've tried I have been unable to locate him since.

57

ANOTHER CELEBRATION

When May rolled around once more, I was preparing for my graduation from Suffolk. I had no intention of going for a degree when I began attending classes. In fact it turned out I had many more than the required credits needed. It was then that I decided not to waste what I had already accomplished, and made the decision to further my education in a four year college. My thoughts were if I got a degree in education maybe I could open a day care school with Jeff as one of my assistants. I debated over which college to attend. My grades had been good, a 3.8 average. I quickly eliminated Stoneybrook because it was too far to travel, not for myself but I didn't want to be too far from Jeff if there was an emergency. I settled on Dowling in Oakdale, only a few minutes ride from home.

Because of my high average at Suffolk I was entitled to what Dowling called a Presidential Scholarship, and would receive it every semester as long as I kept my average at least at a 3.5. Combining that with what financial aid I was entitled to, a small student loan and a few hours a week working in the office that handled all the physical problems of running the school, on a work study program, I was able to cover my expenses. The other requirement was that I register for at least 15 credit hours, 12 being considered full-time. So when September arrived a new phase began in my life.

I was still driving Jeff to all the Islander home games. Since the first season when we'd bought tickets he had not missed a single home game. When I look back now I wonder how I managed it all, keeping up with all the homework, keeping my grades up?

My first class at Dowling proved to be almost as intimidating as the very first day at Suffolk. It was a speech class, and there couldn't have been a student over 23 years of age in there. I mused, *What am I doing here? I must be crazy.* But my uneasiness gradually lessened. I was exhausted at times but was determined to stick it out till the end.

I applied for a special scholarship offered by the State of New York, feeling disappointed when I learned I had been chosen only as a third alternate. Three winners had to decline before I could qualify. Months went by and I was so busy I forgot about it. When summer arrived the bank sent me an application to extend my loan, and before the papers were filled out I was notified I could have the state scholarship if I wanted it. There was no doubt as to my reply.

When I returned to school in September I learned I was going to have to spend an extra semester in order to qualify for a Bachelor's degree in both Special and regular education.

While I was in school, Jeff was working on his Islander scrapbooks. We had saved every Newsday article printed about the team for the past five or six years. He trimmed and pasted till he tired, watched TV, was still working part-time for the town where he had been made a security guard for the recreation program, riding up and down the halls making sure everyone was where they were supposed to be. He was still selling his flowers when the weather permitted, and watching replays on his VCR of games he'd taped while we attended them.

58

CELEBRITY NIGHT

One afternoon while I was at school Jeff received a call from Jim, the Program Coordinator from the MD office asking him if he could help with the upcoming Celebrity Night to raise money for Muscular Dystrophy that they were planning on holding at Oak Beach better known as OBI, We got in touch with Bryan Trottier, and he went out of his way to help, even calling Jeff to reassure him it would be a success knowing how concerned Jeff would be.

The night of the event Bryan arrived only minutes after the doors opened, spoke to each person in a wheelchair, all the young people there and then the adults. He made such an impression on everyone, his actions even more noticeable when two other sport figures who were to participate arrived by limousine, a condition they had demanded if they were to put in an appearance, then stood off to the side, waiting to be approached for autographs. They came late, stayed only minutes and then were gone, making no attempt to mingle as Bryan had.

Jeff felt so proud to be able to say Bryan was a friend of his. Jeff had a "ball" that night, and after a couple of drinks got out on the dance floor and whirled around in his chair to the music. They didn't raise a great deal of money but for Jeff it was a huge success.

59

RUNAWAY WHEELCHAIR

It was a very long hot summer. Jeff was working at his job for the town as he had for the past several years. But things did not go smoothly. In the six weeks of work he had picked up seven thumbtacks in his tires, five of which resulted in flats. It reach the point where I swore, "You get one more flat, and I'm leaving you there." The repairs were what caused the problems, the surgical store no longer made house calls and didn't want to come to the school where he was working. Yet he would ruin his tire if he rode on it flat. I finally when to Patchogue myself and bought spare tubes so I could change the tires myself, a job I didn't relish.

The next to last day before work ended for the summer a picnic was planned for after work at Lake Ronkonkama. I picked Jeff up at the school as usual and drove him to the lake, dropping him off and returning home to panel the front "mud" room. I got so involved in what I was doing I didn't not notice the darkening sky. When I finally did I almost panicked, and drove as fast as the law allowed to pick him up. But by the time I got there it was pouring and Jeff was sitting there soaked, puddles in every nook and cranny of his chair. As I helped him into the van one motor on his chair sounded strange. Usually I let him make any decisions involving getting in or out of places but I didn't like what I heard and told him, "This time I'm going to get you out manually when we get home." He fussed, but I got his chair turned around and pulled him onto the lift and lowered it. Then pushed his chair up the ramp to the house. Once inside, I dried him and his chair off with towels and then turned the blow dryer on the chair and told him to leave it turned off for a few minutes to give everything a chance to dry thoroughly. After about a half hour we decided to test it. Without thinking, I flipped the switch that controls the speed up, or on "high", and suddenly it took off, quickly circling, moving too fast for Jeff to move his hand to shut it off. Round and round it went, knocking the folding doors between the dining and living room off their track, knocking chairs over and almost upsetting the very heavy dining room table. I was right behind trying to reach the switch to shut it off. Somehow in the process my arm got between the chair and either the wall or the table causing an enormous welt near my elbow before I succeeded in stopping it. Thinking about it afterward I thought how funny it must have looked with a run-away chair with me chasing it. Needless to say I made no attempt to turn it on again. I lifted Jeff into his manual chair, plugged the motorized one in the charger and we decided to let it sit till morning. Hoping by then it would be completely dry.

But the next morning before putting Jeff in it I slowly pushed the switch down, on "low" and the chair began to move on its own. I shut it off right away and called Pasco. They promised to bring another chair he could use while his was being looked at. This meant Jeff couldn't go to work that day. I got him up, dressed him, fixed his breakfast, he brushed his teeth, but didn't want to stay in his manual chair, he couldn't go anywhere in it unless I pushed it. Instead he said, "I'll stay on my bed and watch TV until the man brings the other chair." But the chair they brought proved to be too low, and Jeff complained his ankles hurt when he sat in it. So it was back on the bed.

I went outside to vacuum the swimming pool, and I told him I'd come in every few minutes to see if he needed anything. At first he seemed fine, but then he asked me if I could stay in the house. Next it was "Could you stay in my room with me?" I could see he was getting more and more agitated. Then he said, "My stomach hurts, and I'm having trouble breathing." Terror in me began to take over. Those were the exact words his cousin Edward had uttered just before he died. I tried to calm Jeff. "Call someone please," he pleaded. I tried to get Rick but could only leave a message on his answering machine. "Call someone, please," he pleaded again. *But who?* Then I tried the MD office but all they could tell me was they would call Pasco and ask them to fix his chair as quickly as possible. In desperation I filled a glass with about two inches of whiskey, stuck in a straw and urged Jeff to drink. It seemed to help and he gradually calmed down. Not too long after Rick arrived and talked to Jeff, telling him, "You did it to yourself. You almost hyperventilated. You put yourself under too much stress. But you'll be all right now."

Looking back later I realized that was the beginning.

60

THE SLIDE

October came and another birthday for Jeff, he was now 29 and had outlived the doctor's predictions by over ten years. There were those who thought, "He's got it licked, he'll be around forever." We celebrated his birthday by going to Chevy's, a club not far from home, but after one drink Jeff wanted to leave because he was tired. Nothing unusual.

Then when did the slide begin? I look back and can't quite put my finger on it. *Could the incident with the chair have started it all?* Something made me call Rick during the following week, asking him to stop by and see Jeff. Rick came while I was in school, it was a Tuesday, and we had an Islander game that night. When we returned from the coliseum after the game there was a note from Liz who had gone over to her friend Yvonne's house for the night. "Call me at Yvonne's." When I called, she said, "Rick wants you to call him. He wouldn't tell me what it was about, but I know there is something wrong."

I called him early the next morning, "Jeff isn't doing too well. I think his body is finally giving out. His heart is working much harder than it has been. His 29 years compares to another's 99."

I wasn't altogether shocked by his words, I think unconsciously I knew the end was coming. And I knew then that he wasn't going to make it to Christmas. Rick advised me, "Don't change anything you've been doing. If you alter your ways now he'll suspect something's wrong. If it was anyone else I'd put him on a respirator. But not Jeff, he'd freak."

I wondered how I could go on pretending everything was the same. *How could I leave him here alone even for a couple of hours while I went to classes?* I had to student teach that day but couldn't bring myself to leave him. I did leave the house but drove the car a little ways past Crawford's and went in to talk to Mrs Crawford, and broke down completely. I had known it was coming for years, but now I sensed it was close I was devastated. Pat Crawford listened and suggested I call the school where I was supposed to student teach that day from her house. I returned home and told Jeff I started for school but didn't feel well so came back home.

Using the phone in Liz's room so Jeff wouldn't overhear I called Bob in Florida. I had the feeling Bob thought I was overreacting, not an unusual thing for me to do. He had planned on coming north for Christmas, but now I told him I didn't think he should wait that long, and I asked him to call Bill, who also was still in Florida.

After Bob talked to me he called Rick and was told, "Listen to your mother. She knows better than any of us." And when Bob asked about the respirator he told him, "We could put him on one, and if it were anyone else I probably would, but not Jeff. It would be the end." He also added, "It could get pretty bad, I've watched other young men like him afraid to sleep, sitting in bed watching their own hearts beat in their wasting chests. Just pray it doesn't get that bad. We don't want to put him in the hospital, unless it's absolutely necessary. He's better off at home."

Bob called Bill and told him what Rick had said, and then Bill called me. "Jeff should have some say in this. If a respirator will give him more time, he should use it."

"You have been away from home for a long time. You don't know your brother like Rick and I do. It is better not to say anything. I would suggest you come up if you want to see him once more. But don't you dare mention anything about this conversation to him, if you do come."

After Bob's talk with Rick he decided he was coming right away and bringing Cindy and the boys. We planned a party, calling it a late birthday party, inviting everyone we could think of who cared about Jeff. Bob, Cindy and the boys arrived in time for the party that Friday night. Saturday Jeff went to work as usual, and that night we attended the Islander game and a party afterwards held to celebrate Bryan Trottier's 1000th game in the National Hockey League. At the party Jeff was unusually quiet and subdued.

The next day, Sunday, Bob and Cindy made plans to take the boys to the Arboretum in East Islip because they knew I had to prepare a lesson for the next day, when I was to be observed by my supervisor from Dowling. They thought by taking the boys somewhere it would give me a chance to work on it uninterrupted. But Jeff had mentioned to me several times we should go there sometime, so I went to his room and asked if he would like to go with them. He seemed enthused about it so I said, "Forget my lesson. I'll worry about that later." We all piled in the van. I was sorry it wasn't a week earlier because the foliage on the trees had been more beautiful than I can ever remember, but now most of the leaves had fallen.

We walked around looking at everything, and swore we'd come back in the spring when the flowers were all in bloom. Jeff was having problems with his chair again, and I cursed Pasco for causing him so much aggravation. He was afraid to give up his chair to have it checked again after the episode when it ran away with him. After leaving there we stopped at Toys 'R Us, and Jeff bought the boys each a toy, and then from there we went to Burger King for lunch. We had planned on taking a ride over to the ocean but went to the ice rink in Dix Hills where Jeff watched all of us skate instead.

Back home he was very tired, but then we'd had a busy day. I called my supervisor and told her I was considering postponing my observation because of everything that was going on, but because my co-operating teacher had been giving me a hard time she suggested I try to do it anyway. So I ran to the store, bought different shaped macaroni, to

be used for a craft project and the boys helped me dye it different colors.

61

A BATTLE LOST

The next day was election day and the day I was supposed to be observed but was not able to attend. When I woke early that morning and went into Jeff's room, one look and I knew, he was gone. I stood silently gazing at him not wanting to believe he'd finally lost the battle.

I turned away and went to wake Bob and Cindy. "Bob, wake up. He's gone. Jeff's gone" Thankfully the boys slept through everything. First I called my brother-in-law Roger, the undertaker, then the police had to be notified because Jeff died at home, and the medical examiner was called, and those close to Jeff. The medical examiner arrived and began questioning me, "Had Jeff been under a doctor's care? When had he last seen him? Had he been sick? Did he have anything else wrong with him?" To which I replied, "Isn't it enough he had Muscular Dystrophy?" Stupid questions. I did not realize I was being questioned as if I had something to do with his death. Unbelievable. The policeman who came remembered buying flowers from Jeff, and told me, "We used to talk about hockey and the Islanders whenever I stopped for flowers. He was a great guy."

The morning dragged by. By the time the boys got up, around eleven, Jeff had already been taken away. After Cindy told them Jeff had died, they made several trips into his room, returning to where we sat at the table over cold cups of coffee with questions, "What are you going to do with Uncle Jeff's fish?" Jonathan wanted to know. Then after a pause added, "My birthday's coming. You could give them to me for a present." And later, "Jeff's lift would be good for my father to lift heavy things when he's working on his race car."

Jeff had planned on taking the boys to see the Islanders play the Rangers that night, We decided we'd all go since there was nothing we could do about Jeff yet. I had called the coliseum office and asked them to let the players know what had happened. Nickie and Bryan Trotteir called as soon as they heard and told us if we did decided to come to the game to bring the boys downstairs after so they could meet them. A special thrill for my grandson Bryan because he had been named after Bryan Trottier, had heard it from his father since he was old enough to understand and watched him play on TV all the time.

It was strange going to a game without Jeff. Altogether there were nine of us, Bobby, Cindy, Liz, Jonathan, Bryan, my nephew, Mark, Tommy, Judy from next door and myself. We got some rather questioning looks from some of the fans, but others were very sympathetic and told us how much they were going to miss him. We yelled, cried and watched the Islanders come from behind to beat the hated Rangers. Could there have been a more meaningful win? Especially when we learned Jigs McDonald and Eddie Westfall had dedicated the game to Jeff. The Islanders played their hearts out that night, and down by the locker room many of them came over to console us with tears in their eyes.

Of course the boys were thrilled with the sticks Bryan gave each one of them, then autographed their pennants, and when Jonathan asked Trottier what he had written he told him, "Be good boys and eat all your vegetables." It would be a long time before either of them refused their vegetables.

62

IN RETROSPECT

Jeff was laid to rest wearing his beloved Islander Jersey, given to him by "his" team. It took me a good year before I got past the initial pain of losing him, but gradually things happened to make me realize Jeff would always be a part of my life, and almost everyday someone would tell me about what he had meant to them.

At the end of August following his death a golf outing was held in his name to raise money for Muscular Dystrophy and over twenty thousand dollars was raised. The Islanders were well represented with players, some old-who had known him since their glory days, and some new who had only just met him. Patrick Flatley, Bobby Nystrom, David Volek, Gerry Hart, Gary Howatt, and of course Bryan Trottier. Even Jim Picket the equipment trainer. And there were many there who came because they'd read the touching, "Requiem for a Die-Hard Fan' written by Chris Botta in the Islander News.

I was reminded at the dinner that followed the day of golf of some of the inter-actions between Jeff and the players. In Bryan's tribute to Jeff he told of the time he, Bryan was not playing up to his usual level, and when he came up after a rather disappointing performance Jeff asked, "Bryan is anything wrong?" and after a brief pause added,

"Don't worry, just relax and things will get better."

Which reminded me of another episode after a game one night when Pat LaFontaine made one of his rare appearances at the press gate, and Jeff offered him some advice, "Pat, you know what the trouble is, why you guys were not scoring? You were all shooting too high.

You're going to have to get the puck down if you want to get it past that goalie."

A fan standing behind him looked at Jeff in horror saying very indignantly, "Who the hell does he think he is? Does he know who he's talking to?"

And Pat turned to the fan and replied, "Never mind he knows his hockey."

And Jeff glowed with pride.

I remember

The night the Islanders played the hated Rangers, and Jeff was approached by several Ranger players at that same gate, one of which was Phil Esposito, who asked him, "When are you coming over to root for us?"

Who could forget the night after Dennis Morell, one of the refs, had called what Jeff considered a pretty horrendous game, and Jeff told him in no uncertain terms how bad he had been. And the next time Morell officiated a game he asked Jeff, "How was I tonight? Any better?

The memorable night Ron Hogarth, another ref, presented Jeff with a referee's pin to add to the collection he wore on his bright orange hunting cap, a gift from his old friend Frank. Jeff wouldn't wear the pin though, and every time Ron worked a game at the Coliseum and spotted Jeff he asked, "Where's my pin?" Jeff's reply, "I'm not putting it on my hat till the refereeing improves." This went on for some time. Unfortunately Ron didn't know till after Jeff's death that he had finally added it to the collection.

I thought of the tribute paid to Jeff by the Islander organization, a beautiful flower arrangement in Islander colors with a card expressing their sorrow, the visit by Mike Bossy, and his wife Lucie, at the funeral home to say their final good-bye. It was then I discovered what a loving caring man this champion really was. The floral piece from Bobby and Michelle Nystrom. It's difficult to explain how I felt when I went to a game to find Tom Reilly, the Events Supervisor, had had "Jeff" painted in huge yellow letters on the floor in the spot where Jeff sat for twelve years. Or the emotion it invoked when Liz called after I had moved to Florida to tell me she had been to a game, and after so many years they had repainted the Coliseum and Jeff's name was repainted also.

It brought tears to my eyes when I talked to players like Bobby Nystrom, who with misty eyes himself told me, "It's just not the same without Jeff waiting at the top of the stairs."

How could I forget the night of Jeff's last birthday when Greg and Tammy Gilbert climbed the stairs after a home game, and when Jeff told them it was his birthday, sang Happy Birthday to him on the spot?

I thought of the Booster Club dinner-dances we attended over the years, each year sitting with a different player. When a few of the players were traded soon after they had sat with Jeff he began to wonder if he was a jinx.

I won't forget the last dinner for both Denis Potvin and Jeff, Denis was retiring as a player and had always seemed a rather cold distant person. At the dinner he surprised us when he shook both our hands, and said, "I want to thank you both for being such loyal fans for so many years.

I can look back and see how many wonderful experiences Jeff had in his twenty-nine years, and how much I've been able to accomplish in my own life because of the courage and perseverance I learned from him. His "Cup" most certainly was overflowing and in doing so brought much happiness and inspiration to the many that were lucky enough to soak it up.

0-595-22555-1